**Harvard
Business
Review**

on

MANAGING SUPPLY CHAINS

The Harvard Business Review
Paperback series

If you need the best practices and ideas for the business challenges you face—but don't have time to find them—*Harvard Business Review* **paperbacks** are for you. Each book is a collection of HBR's inspiring and useful perspectives on a given management topic, all in one place.

The titles include:

Harvard Business Review on Advancing Your Career
Harvard Business Review on Aligning Technology with Strategy
Harvard Business Review on Building Better Teams
Harvard Business Review on Collaborating Effectively
Harvard Business Review on Communicating Effectively
Harvard Business Review on Finding & Keeping the Best People
Harvard Business Review on Fixing Health Care from Inside & Out
Harvard Business Review on Greening Your Business Profitably
Harvard Business Review on Increasing Customer Loyalty
Harvard Business Review on Inspiring & Executing Innovation
Harvard Business Review on Making Smart Decisions
Harvard Business Review on Managing Supply Chains
Harvard Business Review on Rebuilding Your Business Model
Harvard Business Review on Reinventing Your Marketing
Harvard Business Review on Succeeding as an Entrepreneur
Harvard Business Review on Thriving in Emerging Markets
Harvard Business Review on Winning Negotiations

Harvard
Business
Review

on

MANAGING
SUPPLY
CHAINS

Harvard Business Review Press

Boston, Massachusetts

Library of Congress Cataloging-in-Publication Data

Harvard business review on managing supply chains.
    p. cm. — (The Harvard business review paperback series)
  ISBN 978-1-4221-6260-6 (alk. paper)
   1. Business logistics.   2. Industrial procurement—Management.
I. Harvard business review.
  HD38.5.H3697   2011
  658.7—dc22

2011006070

Contents

**Harvard
Business
Review**

on

MANAGING SUPPLY CHAINS

Don't Tweak Your Supply Chain— Rethink It End to End

by Hau L. Lee

HONG KONG-BASED ESQUEL, one of the world's leading producers of premium cotton shirts, faced a quandary in the early 2000s. Apparel and retail customers such as Nike and Marks & Spencer had begun asking the company about its environmental and social performance. Its leaders anticipated scrutiny from other customers as well, since more of them were demanding that a greater portion of the cotton in their shirts be grown organically. But the crop required a lot of water and pesticides, especially in poor and rapidly developing countries, where Esquel's cotton was grown and processed.

Though Esquel's executives wanted to strengthen the company's already serious commitment to social and environmental sustainability, they realized they couldn't simply demand that the farmers who supplied extra-long-staple cotton just reduce their use of water, fertilizer, and pesticides. A mandate like that could be catastrophic for the farmers and their villages. Most of Esquel's cotton came from Xinjiang, an arid province in northwestern China that depends mainly on underground sources of water. The traditional method of irrigation there was to periodically flood the fields—an inefficient approach that created a perfect breeding ground for insects and diseases. Heavy pesticide use was a necessity.

Productivity was an issue, too: A switch to organic cotton could cause crop yields to drop by as much as 50%. Even though the climbing demand for organic cotton was likely to boost prices, Esquel couldn't expect them to rise enough to compensate farmers for the lower yields. Indeed, apparel companies and retailers had made it abundantly clear that they would not be willing to pay a big premium for clothes made with organic cotton.

Complicating matters even more, organic cotton fiber is weaker than that of conventional cotton and has different physical characteristics. It would need extra processing, leave a greater percentage of scrap during fabric manufacturing, and require chemicals and dyes more environmentally harmful and more expensive than those used on conventional cotton. All this would add to costs and cancel out some of organic cotton's green benefits.

How could the shirtmaker provide the products customers demanded, conduct environmentally and socially responsible business in China, and protect its own profit margins?

Idea in Brief

With the best of intentions, companies up and down supply chains experiment with isolated efforts to improve sustainability—only to encounter a long string of unanticipated consequences, often in the form of financial, social, or environmental costs. That's partly because most firms respond in a piecemeal way to pressure from customers, shareholders, boards, employees, governments, and NGOs. For instance, they demand that suppliers change their materials to environmentally friendly ones or move manufacturing closer to end markets to reduce emissions from transportation. And they tweak their own operations by using compact fluorescent lamps, recycling more of their materials, and so on. Lee's research shows that it's much more effective to take a holistic approach to sustainability and make broader structural changes, as shirt manufacturer Esquel, steelmaker Posco, and others have done. Such changes can include reinventing processes, developing new kinds of relationships with business partners, and even collaborating with competitors to achieve scale. Stakeholders increasingly hold corporations accountable for supply chain partners' actions, as we've learned from widely publicized recalls of tainted pet food and lead-laden toys. Clearly, sustainability is a competitive concern. The core managers overseeing your supply chain must own and tackle it as aggressively as they do cost, quality, speed, and dependability.

Companies up and down supply chains in numerous industries confront the same challenge: A well-intentioned individual action or demand aimed at making a business greener can create a long string of unanticipated consequences that collectively dwarf the benefits.

The mounting pressure to conduct business in a sustainable fashion comes from various stakeholders—customers, shareholders, boards, employees, governments, and NGOs—and most corporations respond in a reactive, piecemeal way. They demand that suppliers change their materials to environmentally friendly ones. They ask suppliers to move manufacturing operations closer to end markets to reduce transportation-related carbon footprints. And they tweak their own operations by replacing ordinary lightbulbs with compact fluorescent lamps, recycling more of their materials, refurbishing and reusing products, using more energy-efficient equipment, and so on.

I call these actions *substitutions:* swapping one material, vendor, location, production step, or mode of transportation for another. Although each change might seem worthwhile, such actions can, when you factor in the unintended consequences, end up raising financial, social, or environmental costs and lead to supply chains that are not, well, sustainable.

Instead, companies—throughout the supply chain, not just at the end—should take a holistic approach to sustainability and pursue broader structural changes than they typically do. These may include sweeping innovations in production processes, the development of fundamentally different relationships with business partners that can evolve into new service models, and even collaboration with multiple companies to create new industry structures.

This is one of the most important conclusions to emerge from an ongoing research project I've been leading at Stanford Graduate School of Business. During the past seven years, my colleagues and I have studied supply chains in seven industries: agriculture, apparel, automobiles, electronics, high tech, retail, and resources (such as mining, steel, and cement). In addition to Esquel, we've looked at Adidas, CEMEX, the European Recycling Platform, Flextronics, Hewlett-Packard, Li & Fung, Netafim, Nike, Posco, Rio Tinto Iron Ore, Safeway, Smart Car, Starbucks, Toyota, Wal-Mart, and others.

In particular, we have focused on environmental and social responsibility in developing markets. Such economies provide the biggest opportunities for improving the environment, but they also entail the biggest risks. The widely publicized recalls of tainted pet food and lead-laden toys and children's belts made in China and the suicides of workers at a contractor's electronics factory in Shenzhen have driven home the reality that stakeholders increasingly hold corporations accountable for their supply chain partners' actions. Given the tremendous environmental damage that the explosion in manufacturing is inflicting on China, companies that source from China should expect their suppliers' greenness—or lack thereof—to come under more-intense scrutiny.

Clearly, sustainability issues are adding complexity and risks to the already daunting challenge of managing global supply chains. This suggests that companies need to pursue structural change much earlier than most currently do. Actions taken by Esquel and Posco, the South Korean steelmaker, are good examples of what I mean by structural change.

Esquel

To manage the trade-offs among environmental sustainability, social responsibility, and business performance, Esquel helped independent farms and those it owned in Xinjiang try sustainable-farming techniques. For example, it assisted them in adopting drip irrigation to decrease their water use and in establishing natural pest- and disease-control programs, such as breeding disease-resistant strains of cotton, to reduce reliance on pesticides. (The new variety of cotton plants also produced stronger fiber, resulting in less scrap during fabric manufacturing than conventional cotton did.)

Esquel also introduced different harvesting techniques. Previously, farmers used chemical defoliants to induce leaves to drop to the ground so that machines could easily collect the crop. The shirtmaker suggested handpicking instead. Even though that would be more laborious up front, it would make for a cleaner harvest, saving the need to remove dirt and impurities later and reducing waste.

In addition, Esquel changed its supplier-customer relationships with independent farmers to be more like partnerships. For example, to enable farmers to invest in the new techniques, it teamed up with Standard Chartered Bank to provide microfinancing. And to decrease their risks, it started to place orders for cotton when it was planted and guaranteed payment of whichever price turned out to be higher at harvest—a company-set minimum or the prevailing market price.

As a result of these efforts, the yields of the organic farms in Xinjiang that serve Esquel more than doubled from 2005 to 2007; today they are the highest of any kind of cotton farm in China. Farmers' income has increased by 30% since 2005. And at a time when demand for organic cotton around the world is soaring, Esquel has secured a dependable, major supply.

The company improved its own manufacturing, as well. It developed new processes for washing, ginning, and spinning organic cotton fiber; created dyes that employed greener chemicals than those used to color conventional cotton fiber; and reduced the use of other chemicals in fabric manufacturing.

Posco

In a bid to make its steelmaking process more environmentally friendly, Posco had for years undertaken a host of discrete initiatives to conserve and recycle water, reduce its energy consumption, and control pollution. For example, it introduced continuous casters that allowed newly made steel to be rolled into products before it had completely cooled, which cut energy consumption by about 10%. It developed water management and reuse techniques that enabled the company to produce a ton of steel with just 3.8 cubic meters of water. And it recycled nonferrous slag—a by-product of steelmaking—by selling it to companies that used it to make cement and other construction materials.

Posco's managers thought they were doing all they possibly could to be green. Then a challenge arose that made them think otherwise. China's voracious demand for steel caused global prices of high-grade iron ore to rise sharply in the 1990s and the early 2000s. Making matters worse, oil prices also shot up, significantly increasing the cost of shipping the ore from distant mines. These trends prompted Posco to join forces with its equipment supplier, Siemens VAI: The companies set out to create a radically new technology that would cut costs and carbon emissions by using cheaper, lower-quality iron ore from mines much closer to Posco's mills.

The Finex steelmaking process is the solution they came up with. It can use cheaper bituminous coal and common iron ore powder, eliminates the need for coking and for sintering, and, compared with conventional steelmaking, requires substantially less energy and produces much lower levels of greenhouse gases and other pollutants. It has reduced the costs of building a new steel mill by 6% to 17% and slashed the operating cost by 15%. Posco has used the technology successfully in Korea and has reached an agreement with the Indian government to build a Finex mill in Orissa.

Figuring out how to pursue structural change and manage the trade-offs may sound daunting, but it doesn't have to be. It can be tackled in a systematic fashion. In the rest of this article, I offer some guidelines and best practices.

Manage Sustainability as a Core Operational Issue

The only way companies can recognize and navigate trade-offs or conflicts in their supply chains is to treat sustainability as integral to operations. They should consider it alongside issues such as inventory, cycle time, quality, and the costs of materials, production, and logistics.

Recognizing this, Nike has made its supply chain managers—rather than a separate corporate social responsibility group—accountable for identifying possible sustainability improvements, implementing them, and tracking their performance. For example, in China, where the company has about 150 contract factories, its supply chain managers regularly evaluate existing and potential contract manufacturers on operational, environmental, and social-compliance measures. As part of this exercise, the managers consult a database of polluters maintained by the nonprofit Institute of Public and Environmental Affairs (IPE)—something many multinational corporations fail to do, according to Ma Jun, IPE's founder. When working with suppliers to improve their operational performance, Nike also trains them to boost their environmental and social performance.

To do all this at your company, start by mapping internal supply chain operations. Identify where environmental and social-responsibility problems or opportunities lie. Evaluate alternative ways to make improvements that may require trade-offs between the two types of performance. As you weigh your options, consider their potential social impact. After you choose and implement initiatives, continually measure their performance to ensure that you've achieved the right balance of environmental, social, and conventional operational considerations.

Rethinking Your Supply Chain End to End

Connect the Dots Between Your Own Operations

By coordinating across every stage of fabric and shirt production, the Chinese manufacturer Esquel cut energy consumption by 26.4% and water consumption by 33.7% in the past five years.

Reinvent Your Manufacturing Processes

Companies often don't think about radically changing their manufacturing processes in order to become greener, but that's what Posco and its supplier Siemens VAI did: They came up with a new way of making steel that not only cut energy use and pollutants but also slashed mill-building costs by up to 17% and operating costs by 15%.

Work with Your Suppliers' Suppliers

Sometimes the critical players in your supply chain are several layers away. Starbucks faced this challenge and decided to forge direct relationships with farmers. Now it gets 81% of its coffee beans from sustainable suppliers, up from 25% in 2005.

Link Up with Competitors

If you can't achieve scale on your own, think about joining forces with rivals, as Hewlett-Packard, Electrolux, Sony, and Braun did when they formed the European Recycling Platform. ERP has cut manufacturers' recycling and disposal costs by as much as 35% in countries where it operates.

With this kind of approach, Esquel greatly improved both its sustainability and its overall operational performance in its vertically integrated business, which includes cotton farms, spinning mills, weaving and knitting operations, and final assembly. Each area has reduced energy consumption through process improvements, recycling, and the construction of thermal power plants; increased use of organic cotton; and decreased use of chemicals in dyeing. These environmental initiatives have also led to operational improvements: less scrap, lower cost, more-stable production, and fewer production stoppages and late deliveries to customers.

Coordinate with Adjacent Operations

Often, an internal operation can achieve only limited sustainability improvements on its own. Its adoption of a new material, component, or technology may require changes in adjacent units. Conversely, customers' operations often constrain the extent to which you can modify your own. For example, if a customer requires you to deliver once a day, you may not be able to fill up a truck, even though partial truckloads waste energy.

Start coordinating efforts by identifying all the overlapping activities. Then, working with the other parties, explore improvements you could make together that would transcend what any of you could achieve on your own. Since your priorities may differ, the metrics to track progress will have to be comprehensive enough to cover the interests of all operations.

When Esquel applied this approach, it found that its individual operating units typically didn't work together to become greener and, as a result, had missed opportunities. For example, in fabric production, a softener and chemicals used to improve seam strength and prevent threads from slipping were added to give the fabric a standard feel. But some of these chemicals were going down the drain during the garment-washing process. In response, Esquel developed a new recipe that reduced the amount of softener and anti-slippage agents but achieved the same feel. The company saved more than 1 million RMB annually, and it significantly decreased the waste discharged during garment washing.

Supply chain partners need to collaborate even on seemingly mundane sustainability initiatives, as the U.S. supermarket chain Safeway discovered when it set out to reduce the carbon footprint of packaging materials for products it received from manufacturers. The company examined transportation conveyances (boxes, pallets, wrappings, and such) and assessed several alternatives, including different kinds of pallets and slip sheets. Quantifying the environmental impact of each with a widely used life cycle assessment tool, Safeway discovered that the delivery frequency, the routing to different distribution centers, and the mix of products on a truck had to be modified for each conveyance. The company then worked with key manufacturers such as Procter & Gamble, Kimberly-Clark, and General Mills to implement changes. Safeway and its partners had to agree on a comprehensive set of environmental measures and goals for tracking progress in reducing emissions, energy consumption, and solid waste produced, along with parameters for standard operating costs.

Examine the Extended Supply Chain

After you've sought opportunities with adjacent internal operations and direct customers and suppliers, don't stop. Turn your attention to your suppliers' suppliers and your customers' customers—the extended supply chain. It's a critical step, not just to identify more-ambitious structural changes that could generate even greater payoffs but also to better manage risks.

Mattel learned this the hard way in 2007, when the discovery of lead paint on its toys damaged the brand and forced the company to conduct an expensive recall. A Chinese governmental agency traced the paint's source to a third-tier supplier, which had sold a batch of leaded yellow pigment to a paint company and had provided fake certification that it did not contain lead. The paint company had then sold the paint to Lee Der Industrial Company, one of Mattel's longtime contract manufacturers. Ignorance about the extended supply chain had left Mattel vulnerable to a single glitch upstream.

To avoid Mattel's travails, map out the members of your broader supply network and zero in on sustainability-related risks and opportunities. Figure out which performance indicators must be monitored to ensure that all members meet agreed-upon standards and targets. For instance, it's clear that Mattel needs to fully see the detailed specifications of the materials in its toys (including the lead content of the paint), the level of quality control efforts, and the results of inspections throughout its extended supply chain. Augment your own audits by consulting government agencies and NGOs that keep tabs on companies' social and environmental performance.

Once you have identified the vulnerabilities in your extended supply chain, you can collaborate with members to make improvements. To prevent a recurrence of the lead paint fiasco, Mattel may have to work with its first- and second-tier suppliers to detect issues early and train third-tier suppliers to keep problems from occurring in the first place.

That said, engaging members of the broader supply network in this manner can be extremely challenging—especially if they are several tiers below you, located far away, and based in developing economies, where secrecy is often the norm. Many companies hesitate to share information about their operating and environmental performance with other members of the extended supply chain out of fear that it might be used against them in contract negotiations or get leaked to competitors or regulators. So, you typically will have to educate members about why transparency is needed and how the information will be used.

To make major structural changes, parties must align their incentives. This may involve altering payment schemes or using other types of incentives—for example, providing direct aid in the form of training or subsidies—so that all partners believe they will benefit from the collaboration. Such alignment is the key to the *sustainability* of the sustainability initiatives, as Wal-Mart discovered. In 2005, when Wal-Mart initially mobilized its massive supplier network to join the company on its journey to become more environmentally responsible, it set aggressive goals for its suppliers to reduce energy consumption and the negative environmental impacts of their production processes. Concerned that these measures would increase their costs without necessarily improving their revenues from Wal-Mart, many small and midsize suppliers in China did little or nothing. So Wal-Mart tried to mitigate their risks and increase the benefits of participating: It invested in training, codeveloped delivery processes that would cut suppliers' costs and its own, and provided guarantees of the quantities it would purchase from suppliers in the medium term. The carrot approach worked. In a 2009 audit of more than 100 Chinese factories serving Wal-Mart, the nonprofit Business for Social Responsibility found that they had become 5% more energy efficient in the program's first year.

The Starbucks Coffee and Farmer Equity (CAFE) program is another good example. Given consumers' interest in environmentally friendly food products, Starbucks pursued the goal of making coffee greener by persuading growers to farm more sustainably. But the company had no direct interactions with farmers; it had traditionally purchased coffee from intermediaries such as farm cooperatives, food processors, exporters, and importers. Therefore, it needed to involve the players throughout its extended supply chain, including the coffee farmers, in the effort.

The CAFE program spells out guidelines to promote environmental and social responsibility throughout the coffee supply chain: farming and processing practices

Winning the Trust of Communities in Emerging Economies

BECAUSE PEOPLE IN THE DEVELOPING world often fear being exploited by foreign companies, they may resist businesses' efforts to get them to adopt sustainable production methods. So firms should make it clear how the public will benefit from working with them.

Toward this end, the shirtmaker Esquel has undertaken a number of educational initiatives for rural communities. Through the Esquel–Y.L. Yang Education Foundation, it has financed the renovation of decrepit schools in the province of Xinjiang and donated small local libraries. Employee and company contributions have provided thousands of children with financial assistance for tutoring, workbooks, and other basics.

To teach the importance of conservation, Esquel created the Eco-mobile Lab, a classroom on wheels that brings hands-on activities such as tree planting to remote areas. Since it was launched, in 2004, it has reached 146 schools and more than 138,000 students and teachers and has sponsored the planting of more than 22,000 trees.

that protect soil and biological diversity and conserve water and energy; worker pay that meets or exceeds minimum wage levels where the farms are located; adequate health, safety, and living conditions for workers; prohibitions on child labor; and limits on agricultural chemicals. It also fosters transparency by requiring suppliers to document how much of the money Starbucks pays for coffee actually reaches the grower, often a small family farmer in Latin America, Africa, or Asia.

Suppliers are graded by independent certifiers who largely come from NGOs such as Rainforest Alliance and who follow Starbucks's criteria. A supplier must score above a certain threshold to be CAFE certified. Starbucks buys first from certified farmers and suppliers and pays premium prices to top scorers and those who show continual improvement. (In 2009, beans from such suppliers accounted for 81% of Starbucks's coffee purchases, up from 77% in 2008 and 25% in 2005.)

Through the CAFE program, Starbucks offers loans to farmers trying to achieve high scores and provides training and support to ones failing to do so. Those incentives have helped the company lock in high-quality suppliers that are environmentally and socially responsible. With less supplier churn, it has managed to lower its long-term procurement costs and reduce its supply chain risk. For the coffee farmers, CAFE ensures a steady market for beans that can be sold at premium prices. So growers in poor and developing countries are given a chance to earn more-stable incomes and to protect themselves from volatility in world coffee prices.

Look Beyond Your Enterprise's Networks

Sometimes sustainability challenges are too great for the supply chain of any one enterprise to tackle on its own. Take recycling. A single company may not have the scale to support efficient collection and processing. If that's the case, the best solution is working with others' supply chains—even those of competitors. When multiple supply chains use the same materials, consume the same resources, or face the same threats, collaboration may bring cost-efficient, innovative solutions.

Of course, it requires careful planning and execution. The companies in the supply chains should have some objectives and interests in common. They must be able to share resources (processing capacity, labor, or materials) to gain economies of scale. They will have to work out the business model—including whether to establish a new independent entity or a joint venture, or whether to outsource the work to a third party. Finally, the results of the collaboration must be transparent to the participants, who in turn must be willing to share the knowledge and experiences gained from it.

In the early 1990s, many European countries set up inefficient systems for collecting discarded computers, monitors, televisions, household appliances, and other electronic products; recycling as much as they could; and safely disposing of the rest. In each country, a state-owned company took care of everything and charged manufacturers for its costs.

The onerous charges prompted four corporations—Hewlett-Packard, Electrolux, Sony, and Braun—to come up with a better alternative. They formed a joint venture: the European Recycling Platform (ERP). Set up as an independent business in December 2002, ERP has collected and recycled electronic waste for 34 companies in 11 countries. Its pan-European reach allows it to achieve much greater economies of scale than individual state-owned companies can, and the competition has sparked ERP to implement lean processes and become superefficient.

For example, HP's cost of recycling a digital camera is just 1 or 2 euro cents in Austria, Germany, and Spain, where ERP operates, and 7 euro cents to €1.24 in five countries where state-owned companies still enjoy monopolies. Recycling a laptop computer costs HP 7 to 39 euro cents in the three competitive countries and 88 euro cents to €6 in the other five.

In places where ERP operates, manufacturers' recycling and disposal costs have fallen by 10% to 35%. ERP has steadily expanded the scope of the products it handles, and its members now include Apple, Dell, Microsoft, Nike, and Nokia.

Sustainability is no longer a secondary issue. It has become a competitive concern and should be handled accordingly. The core managers overseeing the supply chain, not a peripheral CSR group, must own and tackle it as aggressively as they do cost, quality, speed, and dependability. They must engage the entire supply chain as they seek breakthroughs and try to minimize risks. Companies that take such a holistic approach will steal a march on reactive competitors. They will be sustained.

HAU L. LEE is the Thoma Professor of Operations, Information, and Technology at Stanford Graduate School of Business. He is on the board at Esquel, one of the companies discussed in this article.

Originally published in October 2010. Reprint R1010C

The Transparent Supply Chain

by Steve New

THE ORIGINS OF A COMPANY'S products used to be pretty murky. Beyond the supply chain function, virtually no one cared. Of course, all that's changed. Consumers, governments, and companies are demanding details about the systems and sources that deliver the goods. They worry about quality, safety, ethics, and environmental impact. Farsighted organizations are directly addressing new threats and opportunities presented by the question, "Where does this stuff come from?"

Consider the trouble an opaque supply chain can cause. Most iPhone owners probably don't think about the provenance of their devices, but worker suicides at Foxconn, one of Apple's major Chinese suppliers, forced the company to pull the curtain back on part of its supply chain in 2009. It had to quell claims that it relied on sweatshop labor. Another high-profile case, the "toxic drywall scandal," led to class-action lawsuits. The offending product was imported into the United

States bearing no readily available information about its source other than a "Made in China" stamp. And a few years earlier, toy giant Mattel faced a tornado of publicity about lead in toys, which raised questions about how much control it had over its supply chain.

Conversely, many firms make a virtue of provenance. International clothing retailer H&M, for example, declares that it strives to improve labor practices and minimize the adverse environmental effects of not only its suppliers, but its suppliers' suppliers, right back along the chain. Similar claims—once the preserve of a handful of niche retailers—have become widespread. But until recently, customers had a limited view of supply chains. Even companies themselves have often been content not to ask lots of questions about the origins and pathways of the goods they source.

For many products, origin is an essential feature of what the customer buys, even if it is an intangible or a difficult-to-verify quality. Broadly, halal, kosher, and organic foods are indistinguishable from the alternatives—the distinctions are important to certain consumers, but in a blind test most would have no way of identifying them. Few people could actually tell the difference between an authentic and a top-end fake Rolex watch or Louis Vuitton bag. Counterfeiting is such a huge problem because, after all, an ethically made shirt looks and feels identical to the sweatshop alternative. The fact that consumers nevertheless care about ethics and authenticity is indisputable: Provenance is already a big deal—and getting bigger.

Idea in Brief

Few people outside the supply chain function used to care where products came from. Nowadays, everyone from company leaders to interest groups to consumers wants to know something, if not everything, about a product's origins. Steve New, of Oxford University, explores the technology, logistics, and inevitable opportunities and risks involved in exposing your supply chain to the world. The new tools for making supply chains transparent are proliferating. They range from sand-grain-size radio-frequency ID tags embedded in products, to customer-facing online databases that allow any comer to probe a product's history, to webcams that show what's going on at suppliers in real time. Managing such information so that it's accurate, useful, and secure is no small task. But complex as the logistics may be, the benefits to a company are often well worth the effort. Transparency, if wisely marketed, can win the confidence of consumers who are inclined to buy your products and even that of potentially hostile interest groups. An unfettered, granular view into your own operations can also help you identify problems and, ultimately, strengthen the efficiency and integrity of your supply chain. Nonetheless, power that's so accessible can easily be wrested from a company. Leaders must remain on top of the vast wells of supply chain information at their fingertips so that they can analyze—and then wisely reveal—what they find before outsiders do.

Revealing Technologies

Driven by growing calls for transparency, firms such as Wal-Mart, Tesco, and Kroger are beginning to use new technologies to provide provenance data to the marketplace. In time, customers will perceive easy access to such information as the norm. Revealing origins will become an essential part of establishing trust and securing reputation.

The key technologies are not fundamentally new, but they are evolving and blending to unleash new opportunities and threats. Product labeling has been transformed by microscopic electronic devices, genetic markers for agricultural products, and a new generation of bar codes that can be read with standard mobile phones. Combine these developments with the reach of the internet and virtually unlimited data storage, and firms can now contemplate more-sophisticated ways to track—and to reveal—the manufacturing trajectory of their products.

Radio-frequency identification (RFID) tags, well established for inventory management and other purposes, are becoming smaller, cheaper, and more flexible. New generations of tags—such as Hitachi's sand-grain-size mu-chip—can be used, for instance, to label jewelry inconspicuously. It can even be embedded in paper and plastic, making the product's provenance data part of the material itself. And smaller-scale tags—labeled exotically as "radio dust"— are in development.

Just like a paper label, a technology tag can be used in two ways. It can store data directly, in some cases even being updated as the item moves through the supply chain. Alternatively, the tag can simply hold a unique identifier, which acts as a pointer to a vast amount of web-based supporting data. The ubiquity of such mobile devices means that consumers can readily access this "internet of things," gathering provenance information not just at the generic level of the item category or type but for the specific item. If I'm interested in, say, food safety, the technology can tell me not just about this type of chicken, but *this* chicken.

Transforming Marketing

As customers take greater interest in the origins and authenticity of the things they buy, providing them with tools to track provenance will become an important part of the marketing mix and will give producers and retailers new ways to capitalize on brand value. A key consideration is how much data to make publicly available, and in what degree of detail. Many firms have made bold assertions about how seriously they manage their supply chains. Transparency, at a granular level, gives credibility to those claims.

Retail giants such as Tesco and Wal-Mart have used an innovative service from UK supply chain services firm Historic Futures. The system enables textile suppliers to collect and submit information about cotton products, with a focus on ensuring that products are not manufactured from Uzbek cotton that was harvested with child labor. These data are used internally, allowing the retailers to be more confident in making ethical claims about their products. Asda, the UK arm of Wal-Mart, runs live feeds on its website from webcams positioned at a few of its food and apparel suppliers. Swiss textile company Switcher labels each of its products with a code that consumers can enter at the website Respect-code.org to retrieve information about the firms and factories along the supply chain, as well as from ISO 14000 environmental-performance certificates. Another apparel company, Anvil, uses a system called TrackMyT.com to provide multimedia information about the route of its products from raw materials to finished item. And fine wines from the Blankiet Estate in California's Napa Valley carry a code that, when entered at a website, can ensure authenticity.

Giving online-verification codes to consumers is a fairly simple way to make the supply chain transparent, although the effort required can inhibit widespread adoption. New alternatives radically simplify the consumer's job and force companies to rethink the function of labels. Mobile-phone manufacturers are developing a variety of RFID readers that, in addition to allowing customers to pay for an item by simply swiping the phone over the tag, will allow them to link to data about the product's origin, certifications, and trajectory through the chain. Visual-reader technologies for smartphones are already in widespread use. For example, the ShopSavvy app allows consumers to scan for price comparisons, and SnapTell's image-recognition iPhone app lets users photograph media such as books and DVD jackets, then receive product ratings, compare prices, and link to a wealth of other information within seconds. The latest mobile readers, which can scan new-format QR ("quick response") and Microsoft Tag codes, are able to instantly link consumers' phones directly with whatever data—in whatever amount—manufacturers wish to place online. The new formats hold much more data than conventional bar codes do.

Strengthening the Chain

Provenance is relevant both up and down the chain, of course. Just as tracking technologies enrich the downstream relationship with customers, they also shape what a firm expects of its upstream suppliers. End consumers may be concerned with the authenticity and the ethics of the products they buy, but companies also seek reassurance about the goods they procure. The new technologies of provenance will be as important for supply chain operations as they are for marketing. At each link in the chain, data accumulate and can be passed on, at a low cost, to the next stage.

For some safety-critical industries, assuring provenance is already standard practice, despite the cost and complexity. Sophisticated and regulated systems exist for ensuring the pedigree of aerospace components, pharmaceutical ingredients, and medical equipment. But the new technologies are also changing the economics of tracking, as batch- and item-level analysis becomes possible in more industries and for more purposes.

First, such tracking can help ensure that suppliers are not substituting inferior alternatives for approved sources of materials. One aspect of the Mattel case, for example, involved a supplier that used an unapproved vendor to overcome a temporary shortage. Second, traceability is essential for firms, such as Tesco, that seek to measure the environmental footprint of their products. Finally, transparency is a safeguard against the entry of counterfeit components and materials into the supply chain.

The History—and the Future—of Product Labels

The Bare Minimum

Early labels provided little information beyond the brand and the basic contents of the product.

How to Use This Product

Regulations started to require additional, though still crude, information. Instructions for product use, such as laundering guidelines, became common.

Everything but the Kitchen Sink

Eventually, labels were packed with data, including environmental and ethical certifications, as well as bar codes to streamline logistics such as inventory management. They still revealed little about a product's provenance.

All in One

Next-generation 2D bar codes, such as the Microsoft Tag, instantly link mobile devices to product-inventory and logistics data. The tags can also give consumers web-based access to sourcing maps, live video of manufacturing floors, and detailed environmental and ethical certifications.

Sourcing maps can depict locations and other company data on farming, manufacturing, distribution, and other processes.

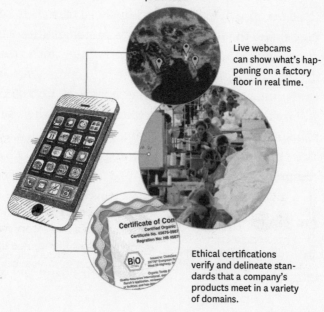

Live webcams can show what's happening on a factory floor in real time.

Ethical certifications verify and delineate standards that a company's products meet in a variety of domains.

Although conventional batch tracing enables companies to work backward and piece together the source of a problem, new tracking capabilities allow firms to load every detail of the production process into an item's record. These data can then be used to analyze quality, safety, durability, reliability, and so on. Provenance and traceability data constitute a gold mine that companies can exploit for continuous improvement. What's more, secure tagging and labeling—for instance, using the new technology of DNA-laced ink—can address product counterfeiting. When integrated into enterprise resource planning systems, item-level tagging allows accounting and costing to be tuned more finely than they ever have been.

Until now, efforts at chainwide assurance have faltered because of logistical and financial barriers to seeing beyond the first tier of supply. Although firms have directed huge, laudable efforts in auditing and certifying their immediate suppliers, the real reputational and operational risks may lie further upstream. Companies will increasingly mandate traceability from their suppliers. At each stage of the chain, a new rule will apply: The only acceptable products are those with a clear, comprehensive provenance.

Anticipating the Risks

New technologies will provide unprecedented visibility into the industrial system. Even if firms opt to keep their provenance data under wraps, they will have no guarantee that activist and campaign groups—or even competitors—will be so coy. The explosion of global electronic communication empowers those who wish to pull down corporate reputations just as it offers firms the chance to build trust.

Of course, access to data would be more limited to outsiders than to the companies themselves, but probably not limited enough to make firms feel completely safe. YouTube, Twitter, and other social media have already transformed how activists launch campaigns against supply chain practices. Witness Greenpeace's recent exposé of one of Nestlé's palm-oil suppliers, whose practices were damaging Indonesian rain forests. Webcams are cheap, and iPhone apps are easy to develop. If firms don't release provenance information themselves, others will do it for them. Scan the code, and customers will be able to see the sweatshop, the factory farm, or the unsafe working conditions—live.

Some companies have built reputations for ethical practices in one arena—for example, certain apparel retailers celebrate the working conditions at their first-tier suppliers. But all firms will find that consumers' interest can stretch farther back up the chain. As Tesco and Wal-Mart have discovered, there is little point in trumpeting the excellent conditions for the stitching of jeans if the cotton is being harvested unethically. Companies certainly should exploit the marketing and operational opportunities that sophisticated tracking offers, but they'd also be wise to reveal what they find before outsiders do.

STEVE NEW is a program director at the Centre for Corporate Reputation, Saïd Business School, and a fellow at Hertford College, University of Oxford.

Originally published in October 2010. Reprint R1010E

It May Be Cheaper to Manufacture at Home

by Suzanne de Treville and Lenos Trigeorgis

WHEN MAKING SUPPLY CHAIN decisions, such as where in the world to locate a new plant or whether to use a foreign or domestic supplier, most managers rely on the discounted cash flow (DCF) model to help them value the alternatives. The trouble with this approach is that DCF typically undervalues flexibility. As a result, companies may end up with supply chains that are lean and low cost as long as everything goes according to plan— but horribly expensive if the unexpected occurs.

You can avoid this trap by complementing a DCF analysis with a real options valuation, which allows you to put a dollar figure on flexibility in the supply chain. This was the tack taken by Flexcell, an innovative Swiss company offering lightweight solar panels for a wide variety of applications.

A small start-up founded in 2000, Flexcell was looking to expand operations after a German investor signed on as its major shareholder in 2006. Like many companies, it faced a difficult choice: Where should it locate its new factory? It considered three options: China, eastern Germany (the location favored by the new investor), and a site next to its own headquarters. The Chinese option was quickly discarded; it would have limited Flexcell's ability to customize its products, and the challenges of getting a distant plant up to speed on a production process involving new technologies were deemed too great.

Deciding between the German and Swiss sites was more difficult. A plant in eastern Germany would have been near enough to permit a reasonable amount of customization, and it would have lowered per unit manufacturing costs by 15%. But the Flexcell management team believed it was more important to have the plant right at home.

Flexcell's CEO, Alexandre Closset, made a successful case for the Swiss location by claiming two key advantages of domestic manufacturing: flexibility in timing production commitments and the ability to directly manage problems. To do so, he had to look beyond the traditional DCF model.

Closset decided to treat flexible timing as a postponement option: If the plant were in Switzerland, he could delay production commitments and investments for several months, during which he could gather critical

Idea in Brief

Conventional financial tools can lead to supply chain mistakes. Most managers use the discounted cash flow (DCF) model to help them make decisions such as where to locate a new manufacturing plant or whether to use a foreign or domestic supplier. But DCF typically undervalues flexibility—and as a result, companies may end up with supply chains that are low cost as long as everything proceeds according to plan but extremely expensive if problems arise. De Treville, of the University of Lausanne, and Trigeorgis, of the University of Cyprus, argue that you can avoid this pitfall by complementing a DCF analysis with a real options valuation. This technique lets you put a dollar figure on flexibility in the supply chain and helps you assess

the value of having direct control. The authors explain how a real options approach helped the Swiss company Flexcell decide whether to locate a new plant at home or abroad. The CEO was able to show his board that the flexibility afforded by a factory near company headquarters would more than make up for the 15% per unit cost savings that would have been realized at a factory elsewhere. He also demonstrated that the costs resulting from a disruption to a Swiss plant would be much lower than those resulting from a disruption to a foreign plant. The decision to manufacture at home has paid off handsomely, especially in view of the uncertainties created by the current economic crisis.

information about demand. This decision allowed him to use the real options valuation framework, which in turn let him put a dollar figure on flexibility. The real options framework also let him put a dollar figure on the ability to manage production problems directly rather than from afar.

Let's look at how real options valuation can help you make sound supply chain decisions.

Calculating the Value of Flexibility

Using the DCF model, you forecast demand (typically by averaging high and low expected sales scenarios), multiply the result by your unit price, subtract production costs, adjust this earnings figure to get an estimate of future cash flows, and discount those flows to allow for risk, using the classic capital asset pricing model. All other things being equal, your decision about where to manufacture will be determined primarily by cost.

But what if all other things are not equal? Suppose that global manufacturing requires you to place a firm production order far ahead of time, whereas domestic manufacturing allows you to wait until you know the actual demand.

Consider first the effect on global manufacturing. When you place a production order ahead of time for less than the maximum potential demand, you are effectively capping your sales and cutting off the possibility of benefiting if demand proves higher than you'd forecast. This reduces your expected level of sales and your expected revenue. The loss of flexibility thus lowers the net present value obtainable from your global manufacturing option.

How does flexibility affect the value obtainable from your domestic manufacturing option? Postponing your production order until you have a better estimate of demand reduces the risk of either stocking out or producing excess. Using the DCF model properly to assess the value thus gained requires adjusting the discount rate to reflect the fact that most of the risk you were facing has now been eliminated. And choosing an appropriate discount rate can be an exercise in guesswork.

This is where real options theory helps. In a real options valuation model, the relevant discount rate becomes the risk-free rate via a simple adjustment to the demand outcome probability. And coming up with values for this variable does not require a series of separate estimates; the values arise naturally in the real options calculation. (For a sample calculation, see the sidebar "Valuing Postponement in Supply Chain Operations.")

At Flexcell, Closset was able to show the board that the value of the postponement option afforded by the Swiss location more than made up for the 15% per unit cost savings that could be realized in eastern Germany. And the decision to locate in Switzerland is paying off handsomely in the current economic crisis, which has caused considerable variability in demand and increased the value of flexibility. Because it can rapidly adjust production levels, Flexcell has neither built up unwanted inventory nor faced stock outs.

The Value of Direct Control

Let's return to the second factor Closset cited in favor of domestic production: the advantage of direct physical control. Investors in commodity markets understand this advantage well. Direct physical control lowers your exposure to risk. For example, bad weather and other unforeseen events can make commodities such as oil and wheat unavailable regardless of contractual supply agreements. Investors therefore pay a premium for physical control. The advantage thus gained, called the "convenience yield," is analogous to the dividend paid in financial markets to investors who own stock rather than merely holding an option to buy it. You can determine a commodity's convenience yield by comparing prices in the derivative and spot markets; it is simply the difference between the value of owning the commodity and the value of having an option to buy it.

The value of direct control over manufacturing-site alternatives is harder to ascertain. Still, you can approximate it by comparing the costs of unexpected disruptions to global and domestic supply chains. The difference is the convenience yield of the domestic facility, which you can factor into your project valuation calculations using the real options framework.

Flexcell's Closset did just that, showing the board that the costs resulting from a disruption to a Swiss plant would be much lower than those resulting from a disruption to one in eastern Germany. For example, if a problem with a new product configuration were to arise in a local factory, engineers could start working on it within minutes, whereas having to get them to eastern Germany could halt production for a couple of days. Including the convenience yield of the Swiss factory in his calculations helped to demonstrate the greater value of the Swiss location.

The decision to manufacture in Switzerland is paying off in this regard as well. Although Flexcell encountered some difficulties while scaling up production, it was able to meet its delivery commitments for the thousands of units presold through 2008 and 2009 because the design engineers and production people were all on site. In addition, the proximity of product development to manufacturing has helped Flexcell take full advantage of its innovative capabilities, allowing it to tailor offerings ever more exactly to customer needs. This enhanced responsiveness and customization provide a powerful competitive advantage.

Having Your Cake, Too

Will applying real options valuation to supply chain projects explode the feasibility of global supply chains? Not at all. You don't necessarily need flexibility throughout your entire supply chain, as the Italian clothing manufacturer Benetton demonstrated in the 1960s.

Benetton realized that many clothes were differentiated by color, not shape or design. So it employed women in northern Italian villages to weave garments in neutral colors and shipped the garments to its headquarters, dyeing them there at the last minute in order to choose colors on the basis of the latest consumer trends. By postponing just the dyeing, Benetton dramatically reduced its overall production risks. The rest of the process could still be fixed far in advance.

One simple intuition was enough to give Benetton a significant competitive advantage. When the choices are more nuanced, however, real options valuation can help supply chain strategists make much better informed decisions about which parts of the supply chain to locate where.

We've focused on putting a dollar figure on the flexibility gained by keeping production close to home. But there are other ways to increase flexibility, of course—for example, by investing in excess capacity or inventory. Taking a real options valuation approach to these decisions as well can help companies appreciate just where in a fashionably lean, globally dispersed supply chain hidden costs may lurk.

SUZANNE DE TREVILLE is a professor of operations management at the University of Lausanne. **LENOS TRIGEORGIS** is the Bank of Cyprus Chair Professor of Finance at the University of Cyprus.

Originally published in October 2010. Reprint R1010F

The Triple-A Supply Chain

by Hau L. Lee

DURING THE PAST DECADE and a half, I've studied from the inside more than 60 leading companies that focused on building and rebuilding supply chains to deliver goods and services to consumers as quickly and inexpensively as possible. Those firms invested in state-of-the-art technologies, and when that proved to be inadequate, they hired top-notch talent to boost supply chain performance. Many companies also teamed up to streamline processes, lay down technical standards, and invest in infrastructure they could share. For instance, in the early 1990s, American apparel companies started a Quick Response initiative, grocery companies in Europe and the United States touted a program called Efficient Consumer Response, and the U.S. food service industry embarked on an Efficient Foodservice Response program.

All those companies and initiatives persistently aimed at greater speed and cost-effectiveness—the popular grails of supply chain management. Of course, companies' quests changed with the industrial cycle: When business was booming, executives concentrated on maximizing speed, and when the economy headed south, firms desperately tried to minimize supply costs.

As time went by, however, I observed one fundamental problem that most companies and experts seemed to ignore: Ceteris paribus, companies whose supply chains became more efficient and cost-effective didn't gain a sustainable advantage over their rivals. In fact, the performance of those supply chains steadily deteriorated. For instance, despite the increased efficiency of many companies' supply chains, the percentage of products that were marked down in the United States rose from less than 10% in 1980 to more than 30% in 2000, and surveys show that consumer satisfaction with product availability fell sharply during the same period.

Evidently, it isn't by becoming more efficient that the supply chains of Wal-Mart, Dell, and Amazon have given those companies an edge over their competitors. According to my research, top-performing supply chains possess three very different qualities. First, great supply chains are agile. They react speedily to sudden changes in demand or supply. Second, they adapt over time as market structures and strategies evolve. Third, they align the interests of all the firms in the supply network so that companies optimize the chain's performance when they maximize their interests. Only supply chains that are agile, adaptable, and aligned provide companies with sustainable competitive advantage.

Idea in Brief

The holy grails of supply chain management are high speed and low cost—or are they? Though necessary, they aren't sufficient to give companies a sustainable competitive advantage over rivals. Consider these disturbing statistics: Though U.S. supply chains became significantly faster and cheaper between 1980 and 2000, product markdowns owing to excess inventory jumped from 10% to 30% of total units sold—while customer satisfaction with product availability plummeted.

But some companies—Wal-Mart, Amazon.com, Dell Computer—have bucked these trends. How? Their supply chains aren't *just* fast and cost-effective. They're also:

- **Agile:** They respond quickly to sudden changes in supply or demand. They handle unexpected external disruptions smoothly and cost-efficiently. And they recover promptly from shocks such as natural disasters, epidemics, and computer viruses.

- **Adaptable:** They evolve over time as economic progress, political shifts, demographic trends, and technological advances reshape markets.

- **Aligned:** They align the interests of all participating firms in the supply chain with their own. As each player maximizes its own interests, it optimizes the chain's performance as well.

To achieve sustainable competitive advantage, your supply chain needs *all three* of these qualities. Apply the following practices to create agility, adaptability, *and* alignment.

The Perils of Efficiency

Why haven't efficient supply chains been able to deliver the goods? For several reasons. High-speed, low-cost supply chains are unable to respond to unexpected changes in demand or supply. Many companies have centralized manufacturing and distribution facilities to generate scale economies, and they deliver only

Idea in Practice

Agility

Objective: Respond to short-term changes in demand or supply quickly.

Methods:

- Continuously provide supply chain partners with data on changes in supply and demand so they can respond promptly.

- Collaborate with suppliers and customers to redesign processes, components, and products in ways that give you a head start over rivals.

- Finish products only when you have accurate information on customer preferences.

- Keep a small inventory of inexpensive, nonbulky product components to prevent manufacturing delays.

Adaptability

Objective: Adjust supply chain design to accommodate market changes.

Methods:

- Track economic changes, especially in developing countries.

- Use intermediaries to find reliable vendors in unfamiliar parts of the world.

- Create flexibility by ensuring that different products use the same components and production processes.

- Create different supply chains for different product lines, to optimize capabilities for each. For example, with highly customized, low-volume products, use vendors close to your main markets. For standard, high-volume products, commission contract manufacturers in low-cost countries.

Alignment

Objectives: Establish incentives for supply chain partners to improve performance of the entire chain.

container loads of products to customers to minimize transportation time, freight costs, and the number of deliveries. When demand for a particular brand, pack size, or assortment rises without warning, these organizations are unable to react even if they have the items in

Methods:

- Provide all partners with equal access to forecasts, sales data, and plans.

- Clarify partners' roles and responsibilities to avoid conflict.

- Redefine partnership terms to share risks, costs, and rewards for improving supply chain performance.

- Align incentives so that players maximize overall chain performance while also maximizing their returns from the partnership.

Example: Convenience-store chain Seven-Eleven Japan (SEJ) builds supply chain agility by using real-time systems to detect changes in customer preferences and track sales and customer data at every store. Satellite connections link stores with distribution centers, suppliers, and logistics providers. SEJ reallocates inventory among stores and reconfigures store shelves three times daily to cater to different customer groups at different hours.

SEJ's **adaptability** is legendary. Within six hours after the 1995 Kobe earthquake, SEJ overcame highway gridlock by mobilizing helicopters and motorcycles to deliver 64,000 rice balls to its stores in the beleaguered city.

SEJ fosters **alignment** by making partners' incentives and disincentives clear. For example, when carriers fail to deliver on time, they pay a penalty. But SEJ also helps carriers save money by forgoing the typical time-consuming requirement that store managers verify all contents of each delivery truck.

stock. According to two studies I helped conduct in the 1990s, the required merchandise was often already in factory stockyards, packed and ready to ship, but it couldn't be moved until each container was full. That "best" practice delayed shipments by a week or more,

45

forcing stocked-out stores to turn away consumers. No wonder then that, according to another recent research report, when companies announce product promotions, stock outs rise to 15%, on average, even when executives have primed supply chains to handle demand fluctuations.

When manufacturers eventually deliver additional merchandise, it results in excess inventory because most distributors don't need a container load to satisfy the increased demand. To get rid of the stockpile, companies mark down those products sooner than they had planned to. That's partly why department stores sell as much as a third of their merchandise at discounted prices. Those markdowns not only reduce companies' profits but also erode brand equity and anger loyal customers who bought the items at full price in the recent past (sound familiar?).

Companies' obsession with speed and costs also causes supply chains to break down during the launch of new products. Some years ago, I studied a well-known consumer electronics firm that decided not to create a buffer stock before launching an innovative new product. It wanted to keep inventory costs low, particularly since it hadn't been able to generate an accurate demand forecast. When demand rose soon after the gizmo's launch and fell sharply thereafter, the company pressured vendors to boost production and then to slash output. When demand shot up again a few weeks later, executives enthusiastically told vendors to step up production once more. Five days later, supplies of the new product dried up as if someone had turned off a tap.

The shocked electronics giant discovered that vendors had been so busy ramping production up and down that they hadn't found time to fix bugs in both the components' manufacturing and the product's assembly processes. When the suppliers tried to boost output a second time, product defects rose to unacceptable levels, and some vendors, including the main assembler, had to shut down production lines for more than a week. By the time the suppliers could fix the glitches and restart production, the innovation was all but dead. If the electronics company had given suppliers a steady, higher-than-needed manufacturing schedule until both the line and demand had stabilized, it would have initially had higher inventory costs, but the product would still be around.

Efficient supply chains often become uncompetitive because they don't adapt to changes in the structures of markets. Consider Lucent's Electronic Switching Systems division, which set up a fast and cost-effective supply chain in the late 1980s by centralizing component procurement, assembly and testing, and order fulfillment in Oklahoma City. The supply chain worked brilliantly as long as most of the demand for digital switches emanated from the Americas and as long as Lucent's vendors were mostly in the United States. However, in the 1990s, when Asia became the world's fastest-growing market, Lucent's response times increased because it hadn't set up a plant in the Far East. Furthermore, the company couldn't customize switches or carry out modifications because of the amount of time and money it took the supply chain to do those things across continents.

Building the Triple-A Supply Chain

Agility

Objectives: Respond to short-term changes in demand or supply quickly; handle external disruptions smoothly.

Methods:

- Promote flow of information with suppliers and customers.

- Develop collaborative relationships with suppliers.

- Design for postponement.

- Build inventory buffers by maintaining a stockpile of inexpensive but key components.

- Have a dependable logistics system or partner.

- Draw up contingency plans and develop crisis management teams.

Adaptability

Objectives: Adjust supply chain's design to meet structural shifts in markets; modify supply network to strategies, products, and technologies.

Lucent's troubles deepened when vendors shifted manufacturing facilities from the United States to Asia to take advantage of the lower labor costs there. "We had to fly components from Asia to Oklahoma City and fly them back again to Asia as finished products. That was costly and time consuming," Lucent's then head of manufacturing told me. With tongue firmly in cheek, he added, "Neither components nor products earned frequent-flyer miles." When Lucent redesigned

Methods:

- Monitor economies all over the world to spot new supply bases and markets.

- Use intermediaries to develop fresh suppliers and logistics infrastructure.

- Evaluate needs of ultimate consumers—not just immediate customers.

- Create flexible product designs.

- Determine where companies' products stand in terms of technology cycles and product life cycles.

Alignment

Objective: Create incentives for better performance.

Methods:

- Exchange information and knowledge freely with vendors and customers.

- Lay down roles, tasks, and responsibilities clearly for suppliers and customers.

- Equitably share risks, costs, and gains of improvement initiatives.

its supply chain in 1996 by setting up joint ventures in Taiwan and China to manufacture digital switches, it did manage to gain ground in Asia.

In this and many other cases, the conclusion would be the same: Supply chain efficiency is necessary, but it isn't enough to ensure that firms will do better than their rivals. Only those companies that build agile, adaptable, and aligned supply chains get ahead of the competition, as I pointed out earlier. In this article, I'll expand on each of those qualities and explain how companies can build them into supply chains without having to make trade-offs. In fact, I'll show that any two of these dimensions alone aren't enough. Only companies that build all three into supply chains become better faster than their rivals. I'll conclude by describing how Seven-Eleven Japan has become one of the world's most profitable retailers by building a truly "triple-A" supply chain.

Fostering Agility

Great companies create supply chains that respond to sudden and unexpected changes in markets. Agility is critical, because in most industries, both demand and supply fluctuate more rapidly and widely than they used to. Most supply chains cope by playing speed against costs, but agile ones respond both quickly and cost-efficiently.

Most companies continue to focus on the speed and costs of their supply chains without realizing that they pay a big price for disregarding agility. (See the sidebar "The Importance of Being Agile.") In the 1990s, whenever Intel unveiled new microprocessors, Compaq took more time than its rivals to launch the next generation of PCs because of a long design cycle. The company lost mind share because it could never count early adopters, who create the buzz around high-tech products, among its consumers. Worse, it was unable to compete on price. Because its products stayed in the pipeline for a long time, the company had a large inventory of raw

The Importance of Being Agile

MOST COMPANIES OVERLOOK the idea that supply chains should be agile. That's understandable; adaptability and alignment are more novel concepts than agility is. However, even if your supply chain is both adaptable and aligned, it's dangerous to disregard agility.

In 1995, Hewlett-Packard teamed up with Canon to design and launch ink-jet printers. At the outset, the American company aligned its interests with those of its Japanese partner. While HP took on the responsibility of producing printed circuit boards (or "formaters"), Canon agreed to manufacture engines for the Laser-Jet series. That was an equitable division of responsibilities, and the two R&D teams learned to work together closely. After launching the LaserJet, HP and Canon quickly adapted the supply network to the product's markets. HP used its manufacturing facilities in Idaho and Italy to support the LaserJet, and Canon used plants in West Virginia and Tokyo.

But HP and Canon failed to anticipate one problem. To keep costs down, Canon agreed to alter the number of engines it produced, but only if HP communicated changes well in advance—say, six or more months before printers entered the market. However, HP could estimate demand accurately only three or fewer months before printers hit the market. At that stage, Canon could modify its manufacturing schedule by just a few percentage points. As a result, the supply chain couldn't cope with sudden fluctuations in demand. So when there was an unexpected drop in demand for the LaserJet III toward the end of its life cycle, HP was stuck with a huge and expensive surplus of printer engines: the infamous LaserJet mountain. Having an adaptable and aligned supply chain didn't help HP overcome its lack of agility.

materials. That meant Compaq didn't reap much benefit when component prices fell, and it couldn't cut PC prices as much as its rivals were able to. When vendors announced changes in engineering specifications,

Compaq incurred more reworking costs than other manufacturers because of its larger work-in-progress inventory. The lack of an agile supply chain caused Compaq to lose PC market share throughout the decade.

By contrast, smart companies use agile supply chains to differentiate themselves from rivals. For instance, H&M, Mango, and Zara have become Europe's most profitable apparel brands by building agility into every link of their supply chains. At one end of their product pipelines, the three companies have created agile design processes. As soon as designers spot possible trends, they create sketches and order fabrics. That gives them a head start over competitors because fabric suppliers require the longest lead times. However, the companies finalize designs and manufacture garments only after they get reliable data from stores. That allows them to make products that meet consumer tastes and reduces the number of items they must sell at a discount. At the other end of the pipeline, all three companies have superefficient distribution centers. They use state-of-the-art sorting and material-handling technologies to ensure that distribution doesn't become a bottleneck when they must respond to demand fluctuations. H&M, Mango, and Zara have all grown at more than 20% annually since 1990, and their double-digit net profit margins are the envy of the industry.

Agility has become more critical in the past few years because sudden shocks to supply chains have become frequent. The terrorist attack in New York in 2001, the dockworkers' strike in California in 2002, and the SARS epidemic in Asia in 2003, for instance, disrupted many companies' supply chains. While the threat from natural disasters, terrorism, wars, epidemics, and computer viruses has intensified in recent years, partly because supply lines now traverse the globe, my research shows that most supply chains are incapable of coping with emergencies. Only three years have passed since 9/11, but U.S. companies have all but forgotten the importance of drawing up contingency plans for times of crisis.

Without a doubt, agile supply chains recover quickly from sudden setbacks. In September 1999, an earthquake in Taiwan delayed shipments of computer components to the United States by weeks and, in some cases, by months. Most PC manufacturers, such as Compaq, Apple, and Gateway, couldn't deliver products to customers on time and incurred their wrath. One exception was Dell, which changed the prices of PC configurations overnight. That allowed the company to steer consumer demand away from hardware built with components that weren't available toward machines that didn't use those parts. Dell could do that because it got data on the earthquake damage early, sized up the extent of vendors' problems quickly, and implemented the plans it had drawn up to cope with such eventualities immediately. Not surprisingly, Dell gained market share in the earthquake's aftermath.

Nokia and Ericsson provided a study in contrasts when in March 2000, a Philips facility in Albuquerque, New Mexico, went up in flames. The plant made radio frequency (RF) chips, key components for mobile telephones, for both Scandinavian companies. When the fire damaged the plant, Nokia's managers quickly carried out design changes so that other companies could manufacture similar RF chips and contacted backup sources. Two suppliers, one in Japan and another in the United States, asked for just five days' lead time to respond to Nokia. Ericsson, meanwhile, had been weeding out backup suppliers because it wanted to trim costs. It didn't have a plan B in place and was unable to find new chip suppliers. Not only did Ericsson have to scale back production for months after the fire, but it also had to delay the launch of a major new product. The bottom line: Nokia stole market share from Ericsson because it had a more agile supply chain.

Companies can build agility into supply chains by adhering to six rules of thumb:

- Provide data on changes in supply and demand to partners continuously so they can respond quickly. For instance, Cisco recently created an e-hub, which connects suppliers and the company via the Internet. This allows all the firms to have the same demand and supply data at the same time, to spot changes in demand or supply problems immediately, and to respond in a concerted fashion. Ensuring that there are no information delays is the first step in creating an agile supply chain.

- Develop collaborative relationships with suppliers and customers so that companies work together to design or redesign processes, components, and products as well as to prepare backup plans. For instance, Taiwan Semiconductor Manufacturing Company (TSMC), the world's largest semiconductor foundry, gives suppliers and customers proprietary tools, data, and models so they can execute design and engineering changes quickly and accurately.

- Design products so that they share common parts and processes initially and differ substantially only by the end of the production process. I call this strategy "postponement." (See the 1997 HBR article I coauthored with Edward Feitzinger, "Mass Customization at Hewlett-Packard: The Power of Postponement.") This is often the best way to respond quickly to demand fluctuations because it allows firms to finish products only when they have accurate information on consumer preferences. Xilinx, the world's largest maker of programmable logic chips, has perfected the art of postponement. Customers can program the company's integrated circuits via the Internet for different applications after purchasing the basic product. Xilinx rarely runs into inventory problems as a result.

- Keep a small inventory of inexpensive, nonbulky components that are often the cause of bottlenecks. For example, apparel manufacturers H&M, Mango, and Zara maintain supplies of accessories such as decorative buttons, zippers, hooks, and snaps so that they can finish clothes even if supply chains break down.

- Build a dependable logistics system that can enable your company to regroup quickly in response to unexpected needs. Companies don't need to invest in logistics systems themselves to reap this benefit; they can strike alliances with third-party logistics providers.

- Put together a team that knows how to invoke backup plans. Of course, that's only possible only if companies have trained managers and prepared contingency plans to tackle crises, as Dell and Nokia demonstrated.

Adapting Your Supply Chain

Great companies don't stick to the same supply networks when markets or strategies change. Rather, such organizations keep adapting their supply chains so they can adjust to changing needs. Adaptation can be tough, but it's critical in developing a supply chain that delivers a sustainable advantage.

Most companies don't realize that in addition to unexpected changes in supply and demand, supply chains also face near-permanent changes in markets. Those structural shifts usually occur because of economic progress, political and social change, demographic trends, and technological advances. Unless companies adapt their supply chains, they won't stay competitive for very long. Lucent twice woke up late to industry shifts, first to the rise of the Asian market and later to the advantages of outsourced manufacturing. (See the sidebar "Adaptation of the Fittest.") Lucent recovered the first time, but the second time around, the company lost its leadership of the global telecommunications market because it didn't adapt quickly enough.

The best supply chains identify structural shifts, sometimes before they occur, by capturing the latest data, filtering out noise, and tracking key patterns. They then relocate facilities, change sources of supplies, and, if possible, outsource manufacturing. For instance, when Hewlett-Packard started making ink-jet printers in the 1980s, it set up both its R&D and manufacturing divisions in Vancouver, Washington. HP wanted the product development and production teams to work together because ink-jet technology was in its infancy, and the biggest printer market was in the United States. When demand grew in other parts of the world, HP set up manufacturing facilities in Spain and Singapore to cater to Europe and Asia. Although Vancouver remained the site where HP developed new printers, Singapore became the largest production facility because the company needed economies of scale to survive. By the mid-1990s, HP realized that printer-manufacturing technologies had matured and that it could outsource production to vendors completely. By doing so, HP was able to reduce costs and remain the leader in a highly competitive market.

Adaptation needn't be just a defensive tactic. Companies that adapt supply chains when they modify strategies often succeed in launching new products or

Adaptation of the Fittest

MANY EXECUTIVES ASK ME, with a twinkle in their eye, if companies must really keep adapting supply chains. Companies may find it tough to accept the idea that they have to keep changing, but they really have no choice.

Just ask Lucent. In the mid-1990s, when the American telecommunications giant realized that it could make inroads in Asia only if had local manufacturing facilities, it overhauled its supply chain. Lucent set up plants in Taiwan and China, which allowed the company to customize switches as inexpensively and quickly as rivals Siemens and Alcatel could. To align the interests of parent and subsidiaries, Lucent executives stopped charging the Asian ventures inflated prices for modules that the company shipped from the United States. By the late 1990s, Lucent had recaptured market share in China, Taiwan, India, and Indonesia.

Unhappily, the story doesn't end there, because Lucent stopped adapting its supply chain. The company didn't realize that many medium-sized manufacturers had developed the technology and expertise to produce components and subassemblies for digital switches and that because of economies of scale, they could do so at a fraction of the integrated manufacturers' costs. Realizing where the future lay, competitors aggressively outsourced the manufacture of switching systems. Because of the resulting cost savings, they were able to quote lower prices than Lucent. Meanwhile, Lucent was reluctant to outsource its manufacturing because it had invested in its own factories. Ultimately, however, Lucent had no option but to shut down its Taiwan factory in 2002 and create an outsourced supply chain. The company's adaptation came too late for Lucent to regain control of the global market, even though the supply chain was agile and aligned.

breaking into new markets. Three years ago, when Microsoft decided to enter the video game market, it chose to outsource hardware production to Singapore-based Flextronics. In early 2001, the vendor learned that the Xbox had to be in stores before December because Microsoft wanted to target Christmas shoppers. Flextronics reckoned that speed to market and technical support would be crucial for ensuring the product's successful launch. So it decided to make the Xbox at facilities in Mexico and Hungary. The sites were relatively expensive, but they boasted engineers who could help Microsoft make design changes and modify engineering specs quickly. Mexico and Hungary were also close to the Xbox's biggest target markets, the United States and Europe. Microsoft was able to launch the product in record time and mounted a stiff challenge to market leader Sony's PlayStation 2. Sony fought back by offering deep discounts on the product. Realizing that speed would not be as critical for medium-term survival as costs would be, Flextronics shifted the Xbox's supply chain to China. The resulting cost savings allowed Microsoft to match Sony's discounts and gave it a fighting chance. By 2003, the Xbox had wrested a 20% share of the video game market from PlayStation 2.

Smart companies tailor supply chains to the nature of markets for products. They usually end up with more than one supply chain, which can be expensive, but they also get the best manufacturing and distribution capabilities for each offering. For instance, Cisco caters to the demand for standard, high-volume networking products by commissioning contract manufacturers in low-cost countries such as China. For its wide variety of mid-value items, Cisco uses vendors in low-cost countries to build core products but customizes those products itself in major markets such as the United States and Europe. For highly customized, low-volume products, Cisco uses vendors close to main markets, such as Mexico for the United States and Eastern European countries for Europe. Despite the fact that it uses three different supply chains at the same time, the company is careful not to become less agile. Because it uses flexible designs and standardized processes, Cisco can switch the manufacture of products from one supply network to another when necessary.

Gap, too, uses a three-pronged strategy. It aims the Old Navy brand at cost-conscious consumers, the Gap line at trendy buyers, and the Banana Republic collection at consumers who want clothing of higher quality. Rather than using the same supply chain for all three brands, Gap set up Old Navy's manufacturing and sourcing in China to ensure cost efficiency, Gap's chain in Central America to guarantee speed and flexibility, and Banana Republic's supply network in Italy to maintain quality. The company consequently incurs higher overheads, lower scale economies in purchasing and manufacturing, and larger transportation costs than it would if it used just one supply chain. However, since its brands cater to different consumer segments, Gap uses different kinds of supply networks to maintain distinctive positions. The adaptation has worked. Many consumers don't realize that Gap owns all three brands, and the three chains serve as backups in case of emergency.

Sometimes it's difficult for companies to define the appropriate markets, especially when they are launching innovative new products. The trick is to remember that products embody different levels of technology.

For instance, after records came cassettes and then CDs. Videotapes were followed by DVDs, and almost anything analog is now or will soon become digital. Also, every product is at a certain stage of its life cycle, whether it's at the infant, ramp-up, mature, or end-of-life stage. By mapping either or both of those characteristics to supply chain partners, manufacturing network, and distribution system, companies can develop optimal supply chains for every product or service they offer.

For example, Toyota was convinced that the market for the Prius, the hybrid car it launched in the United States in 2000, would be different from that of other models because it embodied new technologies and was in its infancy. The Japanese automobile maker had expertise in tracking U.S. trends and geographical preferences, but it felt that it would be difficult to predict consumer response to a hybrid car. Besides, the Prius might appeal to particular consumer segments, such as technophiles and conservationists, which Toyota didn't know much about. Convinced that the uncertainties were too great to allocate the Prius to dealers based on past trends, Toyota decided to keep inventory in central stockyards. Dealers took orders from consumers and communicated them via the Internet. Toyota shipped cars from stockyards, and dealers delivered them to buyers.

Although Toyota's transportation costs rose, it customized products to demand and managed inventory flawlessly. In 2002, for example, the number of Toyotas on the road in Northern California and the Southeast were 7% and 20%, respectively. However, Toyota sold 25% of its Prius output in Northern California and only 6% in the Southeast. Had Toyota not adapted its distribution system to the product, it would have faced stock outs in Northern California and been saddled with excess inventory in the Southeast, which may well have resulted in the product's failure.

Building an adaptable supply chain requires two key components: the ability to spot trends and the capability to change supply networks. To identify future patterns, it's necessary to follow some guidelines:

- Track economic changes, especially in developing countries, because as nations open up their economies to global competition, the costs, skills, and risks of global supply chain operations change. This liberalization results in the rise of specialized firms, and companies must periodically check to see if they can outsource more stages of operation. Before doing so, however, they must make sure that the infrastructure to link them with vendors and customers is in place. Global electronics vendors, such as Flextronics, Solectron, and Foxcom, have become adept at gathering data and adapting supply networks.

- Decipher the needs of your ultimate consumers—not just your immediate customers. Otherwise, you may fall victim to the "bullwhip effect," which amplifies and distorts demand fluctuations. For years, semiconductor manufacturers responded to customer forecasts and created gluts in markets. But when they started tracking demand for chip-based products, the manufacturers overcame the problem. For instance, in 2003, there were neither big inventory buildups nor shortages of semiconductors.

At the same time, companies must retain the option to alter supply chains. To do that, they must do two things:

- They must develop new suppliers that complement existing ones. When smart firms work in relatively unknown parts of the world, they use intermediaries like Li & Fung, the Hong Kong–based supply chain architects, to find reliable vendors.

- They must ensure that product design teams are aware of the supply chain implications of their designs. Designers must also be familiar with the three design-for-supply principles: commonality, which ensures that products share components; postponement, which delays the step at which products become different; and standardization, which ensures that components and processes for different products are the same. These principles allow firms to execute engineering changes whenever they adapt supply chains.

Creating the Right Alignment

Great companies take care to align the interests of all the firms in their supply chain with their own. That's critical, because every firm—be it a supplier, an assembler, a distributor, or a retailer—tries to maximize only its own interests. (See the sidebar "The Confinement of Nonalignment.") If any company's interests differ from those of the other organizations in the supply chain, its actions will not maximize the chain's performance.

Misaligned interests can cause havoc even if supply chain partners are divisions of the same company, as HP discovered. In the late 1980s, HP's integrated circuit (IC) division tried to carry as little inventory as possible, partly because that was one of its key success factors. Those low inventory levels often resulted in long lead times in the supply of ICs to HP's ink-jet printer division. Since the division couldn't afford to keep customers waiting, it created a large inventory of printers to cope with the lead times in supplies. Both divisions were content, but from HP's viewpoint, it would have been far less expensive to have a greater inventory of lower-cost ICs and fewer stocks of expensive printers. That didn't happen, simply because HP's supply chain didn't align the interests of the divisions with those of the company.

Lack of alignment causes the failure of many supply chain practices. For example, several high-tech companies, including Flextronics, Solectron, Cisco, and 3Com, have set up supplier hubs close to their assembly plants. Vendors maintain just enough stock at the hubs to support manufacturers' needs, and they replenish the hubs without waiting for orders. Such vendor-managed inventory (VMI) systems allow suppliers to track the consumption of components, reduce transportation costs, and, since vendors can use the same

The Confinement of Nonalignment

IT'S NOT EASY FOR EXECUTIVES to accept that different firms in the same supply chain can have different interests, or that interest nonalignment can lead to inventory problems as dire as those that may arise through a lack of agility or a lack of adaptability. But the story of Cisco's supply chain clinches the argument.

All through the 1990s, everyone regarded Cisco's supply chain as almost infallible. The company was among the first to make use of the Internet to communicate with suppliers and customers, automate work flows among trading partners, and use solutions such as remote product testing, which allowed suppliers to deliver quality results with a minimum of manual input. Cisco outsourced the manufacturing of most of its networking products and worked closely with contract manufacturers to select the right locations to support its needs. If ever there were a supply chain that was agile and adaptable, Cisco's was it.

Why then did Cisco have to write off $2.25 billion of inventory in 2001? There were several factors at play, but the main culprit was the misalignment of Cisco's interests with those of its contract manufacturers. The contractors accumulated a large amount of inventory for months without factoring in the demand for Cisco's products. Even when the growth of the U.S. economy slowed down, the contractors continued to produce and store inventory at the same pace. Finally, Cisco found it couldn't use most of the inventory of raw materials because demand had fallen sharply. The company had to sell the raw materials off as scrap.

---

hub to support several manufacturers, derive scale benefits. When VMI offers so many advantages, why hasn't it always reduced costs?

The problem starts with the fact that suppliers own components until they physically enter the manufacturers' assembly plants and therefore bear the costs of inventories for longer periods than they used to. Many suppliers are small and medium-sized companies that must borrow money to finance inventories at higher interest rates than large manufacturers pay. Thus, manufacturers have reduced costs by shifting the ownership of inventories to vendors, but supply chains bear higher costs because vendors' costs have risen. In fact, some VMI systems have generated friction because manufacturers have refused to share costs with vendors.

One way companies align their partners' interests with their own is by redefining the terms of their relationships so that firms share risks, costs, and rewards equitably. For instance, the world's largest printer, RR Donnelley (which prints this magazine) recognized in the late 1990s that its supply chain performance relied heavily on paper-and-ink suppliers. If the quality and reliability of supplies improved, the company could reduce waste and make deliveries to customers on time. Like many other firms, RR Donnelley encouraged suppliers to come up with suggestions for improving processes and products. To align their interests with its own, however, the company also offered to split any resulting savings with suppliers. Not surprisingly, supplier-initiated improvements have helped enhance RR Donnelley's supply chain ever since.

Sometimes the process of alignment involves the use of intermediaries. In the case of VMI, for instance, some financial institutions now buy components from suppliers at hubs and sell them to manufacturers. Everyone benefits because the intermediaries' financing costs are lower than the vendors' costs. Although such an arrangement requires trust and commitment on the part of suppliers, financial intermediaries, and manufacturers, it is a powerful way to align the interests of companies in supply chains.

Automaker Saturn's service parts supply chain, one of the best in the industry, is a great example of incentive alignment that has led to outstanding results. Instead of causing heartburn, the system works well because Saturn aligned the interests of everyone in the chain—especially consumers.

Saturn has relieved car dealers of the burden of managing service parts inventories. The company uses a central system to make stocking and replenishment decisions for dealers, who have the right to accept, reject, or modify the company's suggestions. Saturn doesn't just monitor its performance in delivering service parts to dealers, even though that is the company's only responsibility. Instead, Saturn holds its managers and the dealers jointly accountable for the quality of service the vehicle owners experience. For example, the company tracks the off-the-shelf availability of parts at the dealers as the relevant metric. Saturn also measures its Service Parts Operation (SPO) division on the profits that dealers make from service parts as well as on the number of emergency orders that dealers place. That's because when a dealer doesn't have a part, Saturn transfers it from another dealer and bears the shipping costs. The SPO division can't overstock dealers because Saturn shares the costs of excess inventory with them. If no one buys a particular part from a dealer for nine months, Saturn will buy it back as obsolete inventory.

That kind of alignment produces two results. First, everyone in the chain has the same objective: to deliver the best service to consumers. While the off-the-shelf availability of service parts in the automobile industry ranges from 70% to 80%, service part availability at Saturn's dealers is 92.5%. After taking transfers from other retailers into account, the same-day availability of spare parts is actually 94%. Second, the right to decide about inventory replenishment rests with Saturn, which is in the best position to make those decisions. The company shares the risks of stock outs or overstocks with dealers, so it has an interest in making the best possible decisions. Fittingly, the inventory turnover (a measure of how efficient inventory management is, calculated by dividing the annual cost of inventory sold by the average inventory) of spare parts at Saturn's dealers is seven times a year while it is only between one and five times a year for other automobile companies' dealers.

Like Saturn, clever companies create alignment in supply chains in several ways. They start with the alignment of information, so that all the companies in a supply chain have equal access to forecasts, sales data, and plans. Next they align identities; in other words, the manufacturer must define the roles and responsibilities of each partner so that there is no scope for conflict. Then companies must align incentives, so that when companies try to maximize returns, they also maximize the supply chain's performance. To ensure that happens, companies must try to predict the possible behavior of supply chain partners in the light of their current incentives. Companies often perform such analyses to predict what competitors would do if they raised prices or entered a new segment; they need to do the same with their supply chain partners. Then they must redesign incentives so partners act in ways that are closer to what's best for the entire supply chain.

Seven-Eleven Japan's Three Aces

Seven-Eleven Japan (SEJ) is an example of how a company that builds its supply chain on agility, adaptability, and alignment stays ahead of its rivals. The $21 billion convenience store chain has remarkably low stock out rates and in 2004 had an inventory turnover of 55. With gross profit margins of 30%, SEJ is also one of the most profitable retailers in the world. Just how has the 9,000-store retailer managed to sustain performance for more than a decade?

The company has designed its supply chain to respond to quick changes in demand—not to focus on fast or cheap deliveries. It has invested in real-time systems to detect changes in customer preference and tracks data on sales and consumers (gender and age) at every store. Well before the Internet era began, SEJ used satellite connections and ISDN lines to link all its stores with distribution centers, suppliers, and logistics providers. The data allow the supply chain to detect fluctuations in demand between stores, to alert suppliers to potential shifts in requirements, to help reallocate inventory among stores, and to ensure that the company restocks at the right time. SEJ schedules deliveries to each store within a ten-minute margin. If a truck is late by more than 30 minutes, the carrier has to pay a penalty equal to the gross margin of the products carried to the store. Employees reconfigure store shelves at least three times daily so that storefronts cater to different consumer segments and demands at different hours.

SEJ has adapted its supply chain to its strategy over time. Some years ago, the company decided to concentrate stores in key locations instead of building outlets all over the country. But doing so increased the possibility of traffic congestion every time the company replenished stores. The problem became more acute when SEJ decided to resupply stores three or more times a day. To minimize delays due to traffic snarls, the company adapted its distribution system. It asked its suppliers from the same region to consolidate shipments in a single truck instead of using several of them. That minimized the number of trucks going to its distribution centers, which is where SEJ cross-docks products for delivery to stores. The company has also expanded the kinds of vehicles it uses from trucks to motorcycles, boats, and even helicopters. The effectiveness of the company's logistics system is legendary. Less than six hours after the Kobe earthquake on January 17, 1995, when relief trucks were crawling at two miles per hour on the highways, SEJ used seven helicopters and 125 motorcycles to deliver 64,000 rice balls to the city.

Fundamental to the supply chain's operation is the close alignment between Seven-Eleven Japan's interests and those of its partners. The incentives and disincentives are clear: Make Seven-Eleven Japan successful, and share the rewards. Fail to deliver on time, and pay a penalty. That may seem harsh, but the company balances the equation by trusting its partners. For instance, when carriers deliver products to stores, no one verifies the truck's contents. That allows carriers to save time and money, since drivers don't have to wait after dropping off merchandise.

When Seven-Eleven Japan spots business opportunities, it works with suppliers to develop products and shares revenues with them. For instance, two years ago, SEJ created an e-commerce company, 7dream.com, with six partners. The new organization allows consumers to order products online or through kiosks at SEJ stores and pick up the merchandise at any Seven-Eleven. The partners benefit from SEJ's logistics network, which delivers products to stores efficiently, as well as from the convenient location of stores. By encouraging partners to set up multimedia kiosks to produce games, tickets, or CDs in its shops, Seven-Eleven Japan has become a manufacturing outlet for partners. The company could not have aligned the interests of its partners more closely with those of its own.

When I describe the triple-A supply chain to companies, most of them immediately assume it will require more technology and investment. Nothing could be further from the truth. Most firms already have the infrastructure in place to create triple-A supply chains. What they need is a fresh attitude and a new culture to get their supply chains to deliver triple-A performance. Companies must give up the efficiency mind-set, which is counterproductive; be prepared to keep changing networks; and, instead of looking out for their interests alone, take responsibility for the entire chain. This can be challenging for companies because there are no technologies that can do those things; only managers can make them happen.

HAU L. LEE is the Thoma Professor of Operations, Information, and Technology at Stanford Graduate School of Business.

Originally published in October 2004. Reprint R0410F

Are You the Weakest Link in Your Company's Supply Chain?

by Reuben E. Slone, John T. Mentzer, and J. Paul Dittmann

A SUPPLY CHAIN EXECUTIVE WALKED the long hallway to his CEO's office one afternoon, quickly marshaling the arguments he would use to advocate for a global sales and operations planning, or S&OP, process. The goal: Convince the CEO that S&OP is indispensable to creating a world-class global supply chain, which in turn would become a major competitive advantage for the company. It seemed like a straightforward exercise, and the supply chain executive was prepared for any questions or challenges the CEO might throw at him. But as he neared the boss's office, questions of his own leaped to mind: "Why do I have to sell this plan? Why is the CEO not demanding it from me? I ought to be explaining why we're not moving faster rather than justifying S&OP in the first place!"

The answer to the supply chain executive's question is a surprisingly common one: He was not being pushed to move faster because his CEO didn't appreciate the business-critical nature of the supply chain operation. This lack of awareness was almost incomprehensible to the executive—yet there it was. (Perhaps, he thought, it was a failing of his own skills as a leader and advocate.) He knew, of course, that many worthy priorities compete for the CEO's attention and that not all of them manage to gain it. Still, in an industry where supply chain excellence is decisively important for operational efficiency, working-capital management, and ultimately the bottom line, a CEO ought to be fully engaged in this part of the business. Naturally, in some industries, supply chain excellence doesn't matter nearly as much. "But this isn't one of them," the executive thought.

Every conversation with the boss has the potential to be a turning point, to produce a long-awaited eureka moment. So, armed with the rich and persuasive vocabulary of business opportunity, the supply chain executive proceeded into the CEO's office, ready to make his case.

We have a case to make as well. In this article, we advise CEOs not to become unwitting weak links in their companies' own supply chain strategies. The costs of neglecting important matters of supply chain management are damaging to any type of business for which

Idea in Brief

Do you know how your company's supply chain is performing? If not, you risk alienating customers and suppliers, eroding shareholder value, and losing control of your fixed costs. These are dangerous mistakes, especially in manufacturing, retail, or distribution, where a poorly managed supply chain can put you out of business.

To turn your supply chain into a powerful competitive weapon, you need to apply six key practices, advise Slone, Mentzer, and Dittmann. These include hiring only top-notch supply chain professionals, staying current on supply chain technologies, and establishing rewards and incentives that encourage employees and vendors to support your supply chain goals.

Supply chain management is a complex, technology-driven discipline that reaches across functions, business processes, and corporate boundaries. Master these authors' recommendations, and you deftly handle that complexity, ensuring your supply chain delivers as it should.

SCM is potentially a competitive differentiator (most notably, manufacturing, retail, and distribution). CEOs should get involved.

We have divided the supply chain domain into seven key areas where CEOs can exert either a positive or a negative influence. Each area is illuminated with real-world examples, taken largely from our confidential conversations with CEOs, supply chain executives, and other business leaders. We also illustrate the increase in return on assets that a CEO-led reform of the supply chain activity can yield (see the exhibit "The supply chain value chain"). Finally, we present a self-evaluation tool, encompassing the seven key areas, that CEOs can use to assess their level of engagement in and understanding of SCM issues.

Idea in Practice

Slone, Mentzer, and Dittmann suggest these practices for smart supply chain management.

Pick the right leaders. Supply chain management can't be competently managed by the uninitiated. Ensure senior supply chain executives have a background in SCM, through formal education, significant experience, or both. Extend this best-and-brightest principle down to entry-level hiring.

Initiate benchmarking and select metrics. Conduct external best-practice benchmarking on key aspects of supply chain performance, such as inventory turns, availability of goods, and SKU system costs. Set goals for metrics based on benchmarking. Define metrics in ways that generate useful information; for example, "good availability" means orders delivered to customers on time.

Set incentives. Establish rewards encouraging suppliers and employees to support your supply chain goals.

Example: A manufacturer's CEO created an annual million-dollar bonus pool to reward employees who contributed to saving $3 million a year through reform of the company's supply chain. The first year of the plan, employees' cooperation netted savings of $3.75 million. The company also gained suppliers' support for the reforms by sharing, 50/50, savings attributable to suppliers' efforts.

Keep up with technology and trends. Stay current with supply chain technology advances (such as software and devices supporting production planning, inventory management, and warehousing) and process

Picking the Right Leaders

A CEO would never appoint a person with little or no manufacturing background to become the senior leader responsible for manufacturing. Nor would on-the-job training ever be appropriate for the head of sales or finance. Yet, we know of several large companies where tools (such as Six Sigma) applied to the entire supply chain. Understand how your firm is currently using technologies, and ask challenging questions before adopting new tools.

Factor supply chain management into business plans. Make supply chain considerations core components of operations, sales and marketing planning, as well as contract negotiations with customers and partners. Watch for inconsistencies undermining your strategic aims.

Example: A railroad's terminals are evaluated only on how many railcars are moved with each available locomotive. Terminal managers are not encouraged to think strategically about where their high-value orders are. If the railway's most profitable customers' materials happen to be on shorter trains, they sit. In one case, goods shipped by a $100 million customer regularly missed delivery because locomotives were diverted to longer trains loaded with marginally profitable goods.

Resist the tyranny of short-term thinking. Discourage use of deep discounts at quarter's end to "make the numbers." Discounts train your supply chain partners to delay buying until the end of each quarter. That triggers low sales in the first two months of the next quarter, which prompts more discounts. The cost to you: overtime during heavy buying, wasted labor during slow months, and higher inventory costs before the next "surge."

the senior supply chain person came into that role with no supply chain background whatsoever.

We conducted an informal poll of 27 supply chain executives working at large manufacturers and retailers, and found that five had majored in supply chain management as undergraduates, four others had earned MBAs in the field, and five more had taken SCM

The supply chain value chain

One measurable benefit of improving supply chain management is an increase in return on assets. A major global chemical company substantially increased its ROA by aligning functional activities with supply chain strategy. Here are the hard numbers associated with the firm's function-related improvements in SCM.

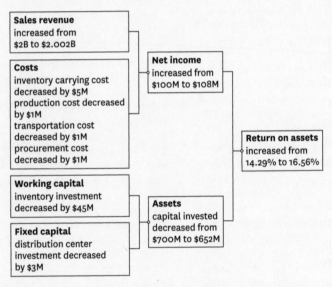

Sales revenue
increased from
$2B to $2.002B

Costs
inventory carrying cost
decreased by $5M
production cost decreased
by $1M
transportation cost
decreased by $1M
procurement cost
decreased by $1M

Net income
increased from
$100M to $108M

Working capital
inventory investment
decreased by $45M

Fixed capital
distribution center
investment decreased
by $3M

Assets
capital invested
decreased from
$700M to $652M

Return on assets
increased from
14.29% to 16.56%

Return on assets was calculated as follows: $100M / $700M = 14.29%; $108M / $652M = 16.56%.

executive development courses. The other 13 supply chain executives had no training or experience in the discipline before they took on their assignments.

What explains this misguided trend? We believe that many CEOs fail to realize that supply chain has become such a complicated set of activities—touching many business functions and processes, reaching beyond the enterprise, powered by fast-changing technologies, and presenting a range of strategic opportunities—that it can't be competently managed by the uninitiated, no matter how generally capable they might be. Senior supply chain executives need to have a background in SCM: formal education, significant prior experience, or both.

Consider the following unexceptional illustration of the risks when CEOs don't recognize this need. At a major durable goods company, one of the very talented rising stars moved from marketing to lead the supply chain function. He was being groomed for a much larger role in the corporation, and this assignment was deemed to suit his background well. Unfortunately, shortly after he took over, an abrupt swing in demand, coupled with a major problem in introducing a few new products, triggered a crisis that put the supply of an entire product line at risk. An experienced supply chain person would have seen the problem immediately and reacted aggressively. In this case, however, no appropriate action was taken for nearly two months—far too long to avert a major disruption in supply for the firm's customers. The impact on performance was severe, and the new leader of the function found himself climbing a near-vertical learning curve in the midst of a major crisis—clearly a prescription for disaster. Within a year the rising star, now tarnished, was moved to another area. The CEO learned from this experience and brought in a seasoned SCM expert from outside the company to set matters right. Within another year's time, the supply chain area had been turned around.

Only a CEO who is up to date on supply chain practices and trends can properly evaluate a supply chain executive's performance. We know of CEOs who, lacking this insight, have retained executives whose knowledge is years out of date. As long as SCM remains a black box to the CEO, so too will a supply chain leader's possible deficiencies.

Enlightened CEOs should insist that only the best supply chain professionals be hired—and should review new hires, not just at senior levels but possibly at lower ranks, where top-notch supply chain talent is also needed. Companies that understand this reality benefit from it. For example, when I was at Whirlpool, we had the opportunity to hire 13 new people for its supply chain organization. I set out to recruit the brightest supply chain MBAs from leading schools such as the University of Tennessee and Michigan State (read the details in "Leading a Supply Chain Turnaround," HBR October 2004). Leaders at Whirlpool viewed this cohort as its supply chain future—a true renaissance of talent.

The CEO of one textile manufacturer extends this best-and-brightest principle down to entry-level hiring: "Supply chain management philosophy so permeates our organization that ... if we can just get quality supply chain management MBAs to join our company, they'll move quickly through the decision-making hierarchy and never be tempted to leave us." This company regularly recruits at major supply chain management schools—most productively during recessions, when other companies cut back on hiring and top talent can be recruited more easily.

Initiating Benchmarking and Devising Metrics

The most effective supply chains achieve the greatest possible availability of goods at optimal levels of inventory, transportation, and warehousing dollars. Specifying goals for improvement in these areas requires knowing where you stand now. A CEO ought to be able to list and explain the factors affecting availability, working capital, and cost; she should push the organization to do supply chain benchmarking and best-practice analysis—and should review the results personally.

However, many firms fail to conduct external best-practice benchmarking. For example, a large pharmaceutical company was comfortable with inventory turns of about 2.0—even though its competitors were doing much better, freeing hundreds of millions of dollars in cash by aggressively managing inventory and overall working capital. Other firms develop and report unrevealing, internally focused supply chain metrics that may actually conceal problems by neglecting crucial information. For instance, one construction materials manufacturer reported "good availability" if inventory to fulfill a new order was simply somewhere in the system, whether or not the order was actually delivered to the customer on time. OfficeMax used to report in-stocks at an SKU, or company-wide, level— not at the store level. When I arrived as the new supply chain executive, we gradually instituted a process of measuring and reporting store in-stocks the way the customer experiences them: daily and by specific store location.

Many firms measure only what they can assess easily. Few of those we work with know the total system cost of the SKUs they carry or take the trouble to measure the true cost of obsolete inventory. Likewise, we know of few companies that put inventory carrying cost on internal sales financial statements. Even those that include this measure typically count only interest cost, ignoring the other inventory costs of obsolescence, of warehousing, and—most serious of all—of draining investment capital away from other, more profitable projects.

When metrics are accurate and functionally aligned, magic can happen. Whirlpool, for example, put in place a set of metrics to track the effectiveness of SCM in reducing working capital. As a result, the company dramatically reduced working-capital DSO (days sales outstanding) and now is a leader in the appliance industry on this metric.

How should a CEO get involved in a program of metrics? First, ensure that any tool purporting to evaluate customer service assesses the company's performance from the customer's viewpoint. Then, make sure the metric's effectiveness is confirmed directly with several of the company's best customers. True cost to serve, determined on an activity basis, should be part of the CEO's metrics dashboard. Total assets employed, including both physical and working capital, should be measured and analyzed in relation to supply chain performance. Furthermore, the CEO should see evidence that goals are based on benchmarks of best practices and that they are shared cross-functionally.

Setting Incentives for Supportive Behavior

Armed with the confidence that best-practice bench-marks have been used to set appropriate goals and to effectively measure the progress toward them, CEOs should also establish reward and incentive programs to encourage employees to behave in ways that benefit the overall firm, not just their own functions. At one retail business whose supply chain executive spoke with us, the purchasing, logistics, and merchandising managers work in cross-functional teams and are measured—and rewarded—according to supply chain metrics that assess purchasing costs, logistics costs of getting the product to the store (also called "landed costs"), and the selling price in the store. Not surprisingly, these cross-functional teams drive supply chain performance to earn their bonuses.

The CEO, and sole owner, of a grocery products manufacturer saw even more dramatic results when he led the organization through an extensive analysis of its supply chain processes. The result was an ambitious strategic plan to take advantage of SCM throughout the firm and also with its partners. The overall goal—to save the company an estimated $3 million a year—directly targeted the bottom line. The only challenges to the strategic plan were requirements for significant collaboration with six key suppliers and three key retailers, and for major changes in how the manufacturer managed various aspects of its internal operations. The strategic-planning process culminated when the CEO met with the executive team to review the plan's rollout over a two-year horizon. In the middle of this meeting, he paused to observe, "You're talking about putting $3 million a year in my pocket, and it's just occurred to me that I'm the only one in the room excited about it." On the spot, he pledged to create a special annual million-dollar bonus pool above and beyond the company's normal bonus system. Any employee who could demonstrate having played a significant role in the success of the supply chain plan would get a portion of the pool. The CEO defined success as achieving the $3 million bottom-line improvement.

"Any year in which that happens, the special bonus pool exists," he said. He then instructed his three direct reports to devise a metric-and-compensation system (which he would review) for measuring individuals' contributions to the success of the plan and to determine how bonuses should be paid out. Suddenly, everyone in the company became an SCM enthusiast.

The owner of this company was a very clever man. How do you make certain you can clear a $3 million hurdle? You aim far above it. In the first year of implementing the supply chain reform plan and its special bonus, the bottom line improved not by $3 million—but $3.75 million. Employees were so intent on achieving the $3 million goal that they actually overachieved, in effect paying for three-fourths of their own bonuses.

As for those six key suppliers, the CEO of the grocery products manufacturer met personally with the CEOs of each, explained the strategy thoroughly, and pledged that for any year in which a supplier fully cooperated and the improvement goal was achieved, the company would not press the supplier for price cuts. Moreover, any savings to the firm directly attributable to the supplier's efforts would be shared 50/50. In essence, the suppliers were now being paid to help the company make its supply chain strategy work. Similar arrangements were made with the retailers. As a result, the manufacturer now had a supply chain whose six key suppliers and three key retailers all worked in concert—and were rewarded for doing so—to make the strategic plan succeed. Not surprisingly, it did.

Keeping Up with Supply Chain Technologies and Trends

Many of the most-promising supply chain opportunities are made possible by sophisticated technologies that a CEO should take the time to understand. Supply chains today are often densely complex. They entail cross-functional participation (and deliver cross-functional benefits), and they therefore deeply permeate the firm. As we have just seen, supply chains are most successful when they inspire the cooperation of external partners. Major new software advances have enabled companies to optimize distribution and production planning, inventory management, warehousing, and transportation systems. Assorted new technologies—RFID (radio frequency identification) chips and systems, used in ever-more innovative ways; advanced bar codes; and other machine-readable coding schemes—have emerged to make SCM more sophisticated. Moreover, powerful process tools such as Lean and Six Sigma are now being applied to the entire supply chain. Nonetheless, the warehouses of many large companies still operate with 20-year-old technology, producing incomplete and unintegrated information flows and resulting in higher costs, higher inventory, impaired supplier relations, and declining customer service. All of this puts a company in jeopardy.

A CEO who understands new technologies can play the important devil's advocate role by challenging the business case for technology adoption. Most firms that have bought leading-edge supply chain systems acknowledge that they use only a fraction of the software's functionality and an even smaller fraction of the promised capability. An attentive CEO can lend authority to the change-management process, helping to foster user buy-in and making certain that proper vendor support, adequate training, and other resources are in place.

Moreover, CEOs who fully appreciate the challenges of deploying complex and costly systems can help their companies avoid classic missteps. The CEO of an industrial equipment manufacturer admitted that her company had fallen into one such classic trap: "We spent $18 million getting an ERP package up and running in our company, and all we did was bring more modern technology to bear on supply chain processes that are 40 years out of date. I expected this technology to bring supply chain costs down dramatically, and nothing has changed. My mistake was expecting technology to solve a process challenge." She is now leading the company through a major effort to understand existing processes, identify opportunities to improve them, and adapt the new system to support the reengineered supply chain processes.

A large global chemical company uses its S&OP software as a communications hub for everyone in the business and for selected supply chain partners. The system allows for real-time access to demand plans, inventory levels, and the transportation status of various different deliveries—information that in turn can be coordinated with demands from supply chain customers and inbound materials from supply chain providers. Anyone in the supply chain can have read-only access to these real-time data, but only selected individuals have the rights to make changes to forecasts, plans, and deliveries. This system, which sits atop the supply chain processes developed jointly by the company and its supply chain partners, is fully exploited as a competitive tool to deliver product faster and cheaper than rivals' supply chains do. In essence, sharing information with supply chain partners creates breakthrough improvements in performance.

For the company to excel in the technology area, the CEO should be briefed regularly about and have high-level knowledge of supply chain technologies. She should also demonstrate a thorough understanding of how the firm is applying these technologies and be capable of asking challenging questions—and getting the right answers—before any new technology is specified, purchased, and rolled out.

Eliminating Cross-Functional Crossed Wires

Can you explain the role of each of your company's functions in driving results in cross-functional areas? At a large manufacturer of consumer durables, the CEO tasked the VP of marketing with reducing SKUs by 20%. However, the VP believed that other objectives—growing market share, for example—were more important than the SKU goal, so he made no progress toward achieving it. As he put it, "The CEO was not really serious when he said that. If I keep growing market share, he won't bother me about SKU count." Even though the CEO believed strongly in SKU reduction (it had paid big dividends at his former company), he did not know how to make it an equally urgent objective for the VP of marketing. In part, this was because the CEO didn't understand supply chain operations well enough to know *why* it had paid off for his former company. That deficit compromised his ability to persuade the marketing VP of his seriousness.

Inventory is another cross-functional sinkhole. We have seen many cases where the sales unit will not use markdowns to move obsolete inventory because the CEO has allowed sales metrics to exclude the costs of carrying that inventory. The firm then pays the carrying costs and—sometimes years later—the cost of the inevitable markdown.

To avoid such needless inefficiencies, the CEO should be personally involved in developing a mature S&OP process. SKU complexity should be tracked and decreasing, as should obsolete inventory. The operations and supply chain function should be held equally accountable with the sales and marketing function for customer service and inventory. The CEO should also thoroughly understand—so that he can help to harmonize—the interplay of cross-functional and supply chain priorities.

Adding Supply Chain Insight to Business Planning

The old saying that the loss of a horseshoe nail can lead ultimately to the loss of a kingdom applies to business initiatives when key information is missing from the planning stage. Supply chain considerations (and expertise) should be core components of business planning, including sales and marketing promotions, and of contract negotiations with customers and partners. That's because unforeseen disjunctions can undermine the best strategic intentions.

A major North American railroad is currently struggling with this concept. Although the CEO has clearly articulated who the railroad's most profitable customers are, this directive isn't reflected operationally by individual terminal managers, who are measured on how many railcars they move with the available locomotives. This performance metric motivates terminal managers to assign priority status to longer trains, even though that might leave the shipments of the high-value customers languishing for days in the terminal. The terminal managers aren't thinking about where the high-value orders are. If they happen to be on shorter trains, they sit; if not, they move—simple. In one case, goods shipped by a $100 million customer regularly missed delivery deadlines because locomotives were consistently diverted to longer trains loaded with marginally profitable goods that didn't require expedited shipment but got it nonetheless.

Another company's marketing organization ran a big promotion while its own factory was in the midst of a major, complex tooling changeover and couldn't provide the needed volume of product. At a third company, during pricing negotiations, a large customer was promised that all of its product would be served through the regional warehouse network rather than directly from the factory. This added a $15-per-unit cost for the company with no concession won from the customer in return. Why? The negotiators, coming from the sales function, didn't understand the added supply chain costs of the agreement.

The takeaway message: CEOs, if fully engaged, demand that relevant business planning and negotiations anticipate and explicitly address important supply chain ramifications.

Resisting the Tyranny of Short-Term Thinking

Sometimes a near-term focus leads to tactical decisions that conflict with one another, creating unintended— and sometimes costly—consequences in the supply chain. CEOs should guard, in particular, against allowing quarterly pressures to dictate unprofitable long-term trends.

Consider how unnecessary quarterly variability disrupts the flow of goods to the marketplace. In some cases, sluggish sales for most of a quarter are capped by an end-of-quarter surge. In others, goods move briskly for most of the quarter only to slacken in the final month. Both phenomena are caused by sales tactics that are misaligned with supply chain–planning objectives. Sometimes the unintended beneficiary is a wholesaler or large retail customer; one retailer confessed, "I'm building two new warehouses to take advantage of my supplier's end-of-quarter push."

Take the case of a large manufacturer of consumer products whose quarterly demand from many retailers followed a three-month sales pattern of low, low, high. In a meeting with the CEO, the head of supply chain pointed out the extreme costs and supply disruptions created by a quarterly cycle consisting of overcapacity and inventory buildup for two months, followed by rush production and delivery in the third month.

The CEO doubted that anything could be done about it—after all, wasn't that the natural demand pattern? Well, not exactly. The CEO learned that the product in question was disposable diapers, and the fluctuations were caused entirely by his pushing the company toward the "urge to surge." By accepting and managing to the quarterly sales numbers, the CEO was subtly signaling to retailers that when the company was falling short of its quarterly target, it would offer deep price discounts to make the numbers. Thus, retail customers regularly bought a three-month supply in the third month of each quarter, triggering low sales in the first two months of the next quarter, which would cause another discount surge.

Evaluate your level of supply chain leadership

Answer the seven questions in the left-hand column. For each question, assign yourself a score from 1 to 9, according to your current level of supply chain leadership (9 is the best). The statements within each column will help you decide where you fall on the leadership spectrum. If you score 3 or lower on a question, a remediation effort is in order—your firm may be in jeopardy in the low-scoring area. Conversely, a score of 7 to 9 on a question suggests you have a world-class opportunity to leverage. If your total score is 56 to 63, you are poised to drive your supply chain to a true competitive advantage. A score of 21 or lower should be a red flag, especially to a manufacturing, distribution, or retail CEO—your lack of supply chain focus may damage your company's interests. An interactive, multiple-choice version of this tool is available at www.hbrreprints.org.

Question	Scoring spectrum									Your score
	1	2	3	4	5	6	7	8	9	
Is supply chain leadership a valued career path in your company?	• You do not get involved in career planning for supply chain personnel. • You do not understand why your supply chain leader must have a supply chain background.			• You are establishing a plan to develop or enhance supply chain talent in your company. • You see the major impact of the supply chain on your firm's success.			• You have chosen an experienced supply chain professional to lead the supply chain organization. • You are involved in the hiring of key supply chain personnel.			
Do you have a program of customer-focused metrics and best-practice benchmarking that drives cross-functional alignment?	• No benchmarking of best practices is done. • Customer-focused metrics are not in place. • Metrics are not shared across functions.			• Some metrics are shared across silos. • Customer-satisfaction metrics for fulfillment exist. • You understand how each function affects fulfillment and shares accountability for it.			• You consistently push for benchmarks of best practices and for sharing customer-fulfillment metrics across functions. • Customer service is the primary metric; activity-based costs and total assets are also measured.			
Do employee and customer behavior reflect your supply chain strategies? Are the strategies clearly articulated? Are strong reward and incentive plans in place?	• You are not involved in function leaders' formulation of incentives and goals. • You do not know whether supply chain partners have been enlisted to support your supply chain goals.			• You have some understanding of how compensation, bonus, and commission programs might inadvertently harm supply chain and profit performance.			• You actively support efforts to reward employees, suppliers, and customers who contribute to your supply chain efficiency.			

Do you understand important supply chain technologies and IT-powered trends?	• You have little interest in new supply chain technologies and leave that to the experts.	• You periodically become aware of—and are curious about—advances in supply chain technology.	• You have a good knowledge of supply chain technologies, can ask challenging questions about them, and have plans to apply them in your firm.
Do you play a constructive role in resolving cross-functional disjunctions, including those that influence the ability to sell inventory at market price?	• Your company has no sales and operations planning process. • Product complexity is increasing or unknown. • Obsolete inventory is increasing or unknown.	• An S&OP process exists and is maturing. • Product complexity and obsolete inventory are tracked and periodically addressed.	• You are personally involved in the S&OP process. • You hold operations/supply chain and sales/marketing equally accountable for customer service and inventory. • Product complexity is decreasing, as is obsolete inventory.
Do you demand that supply chain expertise be factored into business initiatives and planning, promotional programs, and customer-contract discussions?	• Customers and vendors all are treated equally. • Negotiation with partners focuses on price and product, not supply chain issues. • Internal groups routinely formulate plans without seeking input from supply chain managers.	• Supply chain collaboration with suppliers and customers sometimes occurs. • Some cross-functional planning takes into account supply chain requirements.	• Supply chain collaboration involves both customers and suppliers and is cross-functionally aligned. • You stress that all negotiations with partners should include supply chain issues.
Do you ensure that short-term thinking doesn't sabotage supply chain management strategies and opportunities?	• If it takes an end-of-period surge to make quarterly and monthly EPS goals, you do it regardless of the costs. • You have not requested an analysis of the effects of this practice.	• You have a plan to reduce or eliminate end-of-period spikes. • You are gaining a good appreciation of the negative effects of such spikes.	• You have eliminated end-of-period spikes and now clearly see the resulting financial and operational benefits.

As the CEO put it, "This was a real revelation for me. Babies pee at a constant rate, but our demand was fluctuating wildly. We had trained our retail 'partners' to take advantage of us and order only in the third month of each quarter, when we were trying to make our numbers." The CEO subsequently drove the supply chain to offer consistent price and delivery terms each month, saving tens of millions of dollars in supply chain costs. (These costs had consisted of the combined impact of overtime during the surge, downtime and wasted labor during the slow sales months, and higher inventory costs in anticipation of the coming surge.) The company shared its savings in supply chain costs with the retail partners, effectively netting them better prices than they had enjoyed under the old high-cost, urge-to-surge supply chain game.

Another manufacturer of consumer products illustrates a variation on the urge to surge: the urge to hold back. Demand from retail customers followed a quarterly pattern of high, high, low. This triggered greater production capacity and expenses in the first two months, then inventory buildup during the third. Predictably, it also created operational disruptions for the company's suppliers. The CEO was at a loss to explain this quarterly seasonal pattern, which seemed to affect all of the company's products. Like diapers, the products were staple items in grocery stores, and there was no logical explanation for the strange pattern in consumer purchasing behavior. In fact, analysis showed that annual demand at the consumer level was fairly stable month to month.

In this case, customers were being forced into ordering illogically by the company's sales force, whose compensation program was structured to pay a commission that included a bonus for forecasting accuracy. The sales force realized that their sales forecasts were used to set quotas. The CEO, whose background was in sales, wanted to motivate "rigor" in arriving at these de facto quotas. Motivation came in the form of commissions that were cut in half for any sales that exceeded the quarterly forecast. As the CEO saw it, this would train salespeople to forecast accurately. If they set the forecast too high, they'd lose the bonus offered for forecasting accuracy; too low, and their commissions on higher sales would be halved.

Human nature being what it is, the salespeople were motivated to aim low and then stop selling once they'd hit their cautious marks. Company lore had it that the salespeople were great forecasters. No doubt they appeared to be! The first two months of each quarter, they sold diligently until they hit their quotas, after which they refused to take any further orders from retailers. Why take orders that would earn them only half the usual commission and cause them to lose their bonuses?

The perverse incentives also had an impact on customer service and supply chain costs. Customer surveys revealed that retailers' major complaint about the company was the difficulty (if not the impossibility) of obtaining its products at the end of a quarter. Consumers cited the inexplicably cyclical lack of product availability. The CEO was, in effect, paying his sales force to disrupt the company's own supply chain and dissatisfy its customers—and all to achieve the illusion of forecasting excellence.

Now it's time to look in the mirror. We have developed a self-evaluation tool to help you measure the quality and depth of your involvement in supply chain strategy by assessing the programs you have—and haven't—put in place (see the exhibit "Evaluate your level of supply chain leadership").

What should you do if you don't score well on the evaluation?

- Start by hiring the best supply chain professionals available.

- Get personally involved in cross-functional issues like S&OP, complexity management, and working-capital management.

- Lead the company away from quarter-end disruptions.

- Reward supply chain behavior that benefits the entire company.

- Invest personal time in learning about recent advances, including new technologies, in the supply chain field.

- Use benchmarking and get advice from outside experts.

If you scored well, don't waste time gloating. Build aggressively on your company's supply chain strengths, and dedicate yourself to increasing your advantage over the competition.

REUBEN E. SLONE is the executive vice president of supply chain at OfficeMax and a former vice president of global supply chain at Whirlpool. **JOHN T. MENTZER** is the Harry J. and Vivienne R. Bruce Chair of Excellence in Business at the University of Tennessee. **J. PAUL DITTMANN** is the managing director of the university's demand and supply integration forums.

Originally published in September 2007. Reprint R0709H

What Is the Right Supply Chain for Your Product?

by Marshall L. Fisher

NEVER HAS SO MUCH TECHNOLOGY and brainpower been applied to improving supply chain performance. Point-of-sale scanners allow companies to capture the customer's voice. Electronic data interchange lets all stages of the supply chain hear that voice and react to it by using flexible manufacturing, automated warehousing, and rapid logistics. And new concepts such as quick response, efficient consumer response, accurate response, mass customization, lean manufacturing, and agile manufacturing offer models for applying the new technology to improve performance.

Nonetheless, the performance of many supply chains has never been worse. In some cases, costs have risen to unprecedented levels because of adversarial relations between supply chain partners as well as dysfunctional industry practices such as an overreliance on price promotions. One recent study of the U.S. food industry estimated that poor coordination among supply chain partners was wasting $30 billion annually. Supply chains in many other industries suffer from an excess of some products and a shortage of others owing to an inability to predict demand. One department store chain that regularly had to resort to markdowns to clear unwanted merchandise found in exit interviews that one-quarter of its customers had left its stores empty-handed because the specific items they had wanted to buy were out of stock.

Why haven't the new ideas and technologies led to improved performance? Because managers lack a framework for deciding which ones are best for their particular company's situation. From my ten years of research and consulting on supply chain issues in industries as diverse as food, fashion apparel, and automobiles, I have been able to devise such a framework. It helps managers understand the nature of the demand for their products and devise the supply chain that can best satisfy that demand.

The first step in devising an effective supply-chain strategy is therefore to consider the nature of the demand for the products one's company supplies. Many aspects are important—for example, product life cycle, demand predictability, product variety, and market standards for lead times and service (the percentage of demand filled from in-stock goods). But I have found that if one classifies products on the basis of their demand patterns, they fall into one of two categories: they are either primarily functional or primarily innovative. And each category requires a distinctly different kind of

Idea in Brief

Are you frequently saddled with excess inventory? Do you suffer product shortages that have customers leaving stores in a huff? Do these supply chain headaches persist despite your investments in technologies such as automated warehousing and rapid logistics?

If so, you may be using the wrong supply chain for the type of product you sell. Suppose your offering is *functional*—it satisfies basic, unchanging needs and has a long life cycle, low margins, and stable demand. (Think paper towels or light bulbs.) In this case, you need an **efficient supply chain**—which minimizes production, transportation, and storage costs.

But what if your product is *innovative*—it has great variety, a short life cycle, high profit margins, and volatile demand? (A line of laptops with a range of novel features is one example.) For this offering, you require a **responsive supply chain**. Fast and flexible, it helps you manage uncertainty through strategies such as cutting lead times and establishing inventory or excess-capacity buffers.

Design the right supply chain for your product, and your profits soar. For example, by building responsiveness into its chain, innovative skiwear company Sport Obermeyer reduced its over- and under-production costs by half—boosting profits 60%.

supply chain. The root cause of the problems plaguing many supply chains is a mismatch between the type of product and the type of supply chain.

Is Your Product Functional or Innovative?

Functional products include the staples that people buy in a wide range of retail outlets, such as grocery stores and gas stations. Because such products satisfy basic needs, which don't change much over time, they have stable, predictable demand and long life cycles. But

Idea in Practice

Once you've determined whether your product is functional or innovative, follow these steps to match your supply chain to your product.

Decide Whether Your Current Supply Chain Is Efficient or Responsive

Your chain is *efficient* if you satisfy predictable demand efficiently at the lowest possible cost, turn over inventory frequently, and select suppliers based on cost and quality. It's *responsive* if you invest aggressively in reducing lead time for delivery; use standard components for different product versions; and choose suppliers for their speed, flexibility, and quality.

Correct Mismatches Between Your Supply Chain and Product

If you're using an *efficient* supply chain to sell *innovative* products, or a *responsive* supply chain to sell *functional* products, you've got a mismatch. You can correct it through several means:

- *Change your product.* Procter & Gamble had innovative products (extensive variety, frequent introductions of new offerings, and low profit margins) but an unresponsive supply chain. It began making many innovative product lines functional by reducing the number of product variations and simplifying pricing.

- *Change your supply chain.* Make your chain more efficient for functional products, or more responsive for innovative products.

Example: Campbell Soup made its supply chain

their stability invites competition, which often leads to low profit margins.

To avoid low margins, many companies introduce innovations in fashion or technology to give customers an additional reason to buy their offerings. Fashion apparel and personal computers are obvious examples, but we also see successful product innovation where we least expect it. For instance, in the traditionally more **efficient** to match its functional products. The company used electronic data interchange to coordinate closely with retailers. Every morning, retailers electronically informed Campbell of their demand for its products and inventory levels in their distribution centers. Using that information, Campbell forecasted future demand and determined which products needed replenishment. Trucks delivered the required new stock that day. The program cut participating retailers' inventories from four to two weeks of supply— representing significant cost savings. With retailers motivated to carry Campbell's products and give them shelf space, Campbell's sales doubled.

Example: Sport Obermeyer made its supply chain more **responsive** to match its innovative skiwear products— of which 95% were completely new designs each year. The company managed uncertainty by soliciting early orders from important customers— slashing demand-forecast errors from 200% to 10%. It also shortened lead time by expediting design information to production centers. This approach resulted in more than 99% product availability for Sport Obermeyer's retailers.

functional category of food, companies such as Ben & Jerry's, Mrs. Fields, and Starbucks Coffee Company have tried to gain an edge with designer flavors and innovative concepts. Century Products, a leading manufacturer of children's car seats, is another company that brought innovation to a functional product. Until the early 1990s, Century sold its seats as functional items. Then it introduced a wide variety of brightly colored fabrics and designed a new seat that would move in a crash to absorb energy and protect the child sitting in it. Called Smart Move, the design was so innovative that the seat could not be sold until government product-safety standards mandating that car seats not move in a crash had been changed.

Although innovation can enable a company to achieve higher profit margins, the very newness of innovative products makes demand for them unpredictable. In addition, their life cycle is short—usually just a few months—because as imitators erode the competitive advantage that innovative products enjoy, companies are forced to introduce a steady stream of newer innovations. The short life cycles and the great variety typical of these products further increase unpredictability.

It may seem strange to lump technology and fashion together, but both types of innovation depend for their success on consumers changing some aspect of their values or lifestyle. For example, the market success of the IBM Thinkpad hinged in part on a novel cursor control in the middle of the keyboard that required users to interact with the keyboard in an unfamiliar way. The new design was so controversial within IBM that managers had difficulty believing the enthusiastic reaction to the cursor control in early focus groups. As a result, the company underestimated demand—a problem that contributed to the Thinkpad's being in short supply for more than a year.

With their high profit margins and volatile demand, innovative products require a fundamentally different supply chain than stable, low-margin functional products do. To understand the difference, one should recognize that a supply chain performs two distinct types of functions: a *physical* function and a *market mediation* function. A supply chain's physical function is readily apparent and includes converting raw materials into parts, components, and eventually finished goods, and transporting all of them from one point in the supply chain to the next. Less visible but equally important is market mediation, whose purpose is ensuring that the variety of products reaching the marketplace matches what consumers want to buy.

Each of the two functions incurs distinct costs. Physical costs are the costs of production, transportation, and inventory storage. Market mediation costs arise when supply exceeds demand and a product has to be marked down and sold at a loss or when supply falls short of demand, resulting in lost sales opportunities and dissatisfied customers.

The predictable demand of functional products makes market mediation easy because a nearly perfect match between supply and demand can be achieved. Companies that make such products are thus free to focus almost exclusively on minimizing physical costs—a crucial goal, given the price sensitivity of most functional products. To that end, companies usually create a schedule for assembling finished goods for at least the next month and commit themselves to abide by it. Freezing the schedule in this way allows companies to employ manufacturing-resource-planning software, which orchestrates the ordering, production, and delivery of supplies, thereby enabling the entire supply chain to minimize inventory and maximize production efficiency. In this instance, the important flow of information is the one that occurs within the chain as suppliers, manufacturers, and retailers coordinate their activities in order to meet predictable demand at the lowest cost.

That approach is exactly the wrong one for innovative products. The uncertain market reaction to innovation increases the risk of shortages or excess supplies. High profit margins and the importance of early sales in establishing market share for new products increase the cost of shortages. And short product life cycles increase the risk of obsolescence and the cost of excess supplies. Hence market mediation costs predominate for these products, and they, not physical costs, should be managers' primary focus.

Most important in this environment is to read early sales numbers or other market signals and to react quickly, during the new product's short life cycle. In this instance, the crucial flow of information occurs not only within the chain but also from the marketplace to the chain. The critical decisions to be made about inventory and capacity are not about minimizing costs but about where in the chain to position inventory and available production capacity in order to hedge against uncertain demand. And suppliers should be chosen for their speed and flexibility, not for their low cost.

Sport Obermeyer and Campbell Soup Company illustrate the two environments and how the resulting goals and initiatives differ. Sport Obermeyer is a major supplier of fashion skiwear. Each year, 95% of its products are completely new designs for which demand forecasts often err by as much as 200%. And because the retail season is only a few months long, the company has little time to react if it misguesses the market.

In contrast, only 5% of Campbell's products are new each year. Sales of existing products, most of which have been on the market for years, are highly predictable, allowing Campbell to achieve a nearly perfect service level by satisfying more than 98% of demand immediately from stocks of finished goods. And even the few new products are easy to manage. They have a replenishment lead time of one month and a minimum market life cycle of six months. When Campbell introduces a product, it deploys enough stock to cover the most optimistic forecast for demand in the first month. If the product takes off, more can be supplied before stocks run out. If it flops, the six-month, worst-case life cycle affords plenty of time to sell off the excess stocks.

How do goals and initiatives differ in the two environments? Campbell's already high service level leaves little room for improvement in market mediation costs. Hence, when the company launched a supply chain program in 1991 called *continuous replenishment,* the goal was physical efficiency. And it achieved that goal: the inventory turns of participating retailers doubled. In contrast, Sport Obermeyer's uncertain demand leads to high market-mediation costs in the form of losses on styles that don't sell and missed sales opportunities due to the "stockouts" that occur when demand for particular items outstrips inventories. The company's supply chain efforts have been directed at reducing those costs through increased speed and flexibility.

Although the distinctions between functional and innovative products and between physical efficiency and responsiveness to the market seem obvious once stated, I have found that many companies founder on this issue. That is probably because products that are physically the same can be either functional or innovative. For example, personal computers, cars, apparel, ice cream, coffee, cookies, and children's car seats all can be offered as a basic functional product or in an innovative form.

It's easy for a company, through its product strategy, to gravitate from the functional to the innovative sphere without realizing that anything has changed. Then its managers start to notice that service has mysteriously declined and inventories of unsold products have gone up. When this happens, they look longingly at competitors that haven't changed their product strategy and therefore have low inventories and high service. They even may steal away the vice president of logistics from one of those companies, reasoning, If we hire their logistics guy, we'll have low inventory and high service, too. The new vice president invariably designs an agenda for improvement based on his or her old environment: cut inventories, pressure marketing to be accountable for its forecasts and to freeze them well into the future to remove uncertainty, and establish a rigid just-in-time delivery schedule with suppliers. The worst thing that could happen is that he or she actually succeeds in implementing that agenda, because it's totally inappropriate for the company's now unpredictable environment.

Devising the Ideal Supply-Chain Strategy

For companies to be sure that they are taking the right approach, they first must determine whether their products are functional or innovative. Most managers I've encountered already have a sense of which products have predictable and which have unpredictable demand: the unpredictable products are the ones generating all the supply headaches. For managers who aren't sure or who would like to confirm their intuition, I offer guidelines for classifying products based on what I have found to be typical for each category. (See the table "Functional versus innovative products: differences in demand.") The next step is for managers to decide whether their company's supply chain is physically efficient or responsive to the market. (See the table "Physically efficient versus market-responsive supply chains.")

Having determined the nature of their products and their supply chain's priorities, managers can employ a matrix to formulate the ideal supply-chain strategy. The four cells of the matrix represent the four possible combinations of products and priorities. (See the exhibit "Matching supply chains with products.") By using the matrix to plot the nature of the demand for each of their product families and its supply chain priorities, managers can discover whether the process the company uses for supplying products is well matched to the product type: an efficient process for functional products and a responsive process for innovative products. Companies that have either an innovative product with an

Functional versus innovative products: differences in demand

	Functional (Predictable demand)	Innovative (Unpredictable demand)
Aspects of demand		
Product life cycle	more than 2 years	3 months to 1 year
Contribution margin*	5% to 20%	20% to 60%
Product variety	low (10 to 20 variants per category)	high (often millions of variants per category)
Average margin of error in the forecast at the time production is committed	10%	40% to 100%
Average stockout rate	1% to 2%	10% to 40%
Average forced end-of-season markdown as percentage of full price	0%	10% to 25%
Lead time required for made-to-order products	6 months to 1 year	1 day to 2 weeks

* The contribution margin equals price minus variable cost divided by price and is expressed as a percentage.

efficient supply chain (upper right-hand cell) or a functional product with a responsive supply chain (lower left-hand cell) tend to be the ones with problems.

For understandable reasons, it is rare for companies to be in the lower left-hand cell. Most companies that introduce functional products realize that they need efficient chains to supply them. If the products remain functional over time, the companies typically have the good sense to stick with efficient chains. But, for reasons

Physically efficient versus market-responsive supply chains

	Physically efficient process	Market-responsive process
Primary purpose	supply predictable demand efficiently at the lowest possible cost	respond quickly to unpredictable demand in order to minimize stockouts, forced markdowns, and obsolete inventory
Manufacturing focus	maintain high average utilization rate	deploy excess buffer capacity
Inventory strategy	generate high turns and minimize inventory throughout the chain	deploy significant buffer stocks of parts or finished goods
Lead-time focus	shorten lead time as long as it doesn't increase cost	invest aggressively in ways to reduce lead time
Approach to choosing suppliers	select primarily for cost and quality	select primarily for speed, flexibility, and quality
Product-design strategy	maximize performance and minimize cost	use modular design in order to postpone product differentiation for as long as possible

I will explore shortly, companies often find themselves in the upper right-hand cell. The reason a position in this cell doesn't make sense is simple: for any company with innovative products, the rewards from investments in improving supply chain responsiveness are usually much greater than the rewards from investments in improving the chain's efficiency. For every dollar such a company invests in increasing its supply chain's responsiveness, it usually will reap a decrease of more

Matching supply chains with products

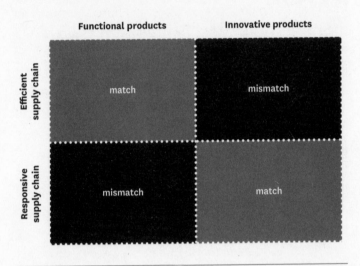

than a dollar in the cost of stockouts and forced mark-downs on excess inventory that result from mismatches between supply and demand. Consider a typical innovative product with a contribution margin of 40% and an average stockout rate of 25%.[1] The lost contribution to profit and overhead resulting from stockouts alone is huge: 40% x 25% = 10% of sales—an amount that usually exceeds profits before taxes.

Consequently, the economic gain from reducing stockouts and excess inventory is so great that intelligent investments in supply chain responsiveness will always pay for themselves—a fact that progressive companies have discovered. Compaq, for example, decided to continue producing certain high-variety, short-life-cycle circuits in-house rather than outsource them to a low-cost Asian country, because local production gave the company increased flexibility and shorter lead times. World Company, a leading Japanese apparel manufacturer, produces its basic styles in low-cost Chinese plants but keeps production of high-fashion styles in Japan, where the advantage of being able to respond quickly to emerging fashion trends more than offsets the disadvantage of high labor costs.

That logic doesn't apply to functional products. A contribution margin of 10% and an average stockout rate of 1% mean lost contribution to profit and overhead of only .1% of sales—a negligible cost that doesn't warrant the significant investments required to improve responsiveness.

Getting Out of the Upper Right-Hand Cell

The rate of new-product introductions has skyrocketed in many industries, fueled both by an increase in the number of competitors and by the efforts of existing competitors to protect or increase profit margins. As a result, many companies have turned or tried to turn traditionally functional products into innovative products. But they have continued to focus on physical efficiency in the processes for supplying those products. This phenomenon explains why one finds so many broken supply chains—or unresponsive chains trying to supply innovative products—in industries such as automobiles, personal computers, and consumer packaged goods.

The automobile industry is one classic example. Several years ago, I was involved in a study to measure the impact that the variety of options available to consumers had on productivity at a Big Three auto plant. As the study began, I tried to understand variety from the customer's perspective by visiting a dealer near my home in the Philadelphia area and "shopping" for the car model produced in the plant we were to study. From sales literature provided by the dealer, I determined that when one took into account all the choices for color, interior features, drivetrain configurations, and other options, the company was actually offering 20 million versions of the car. But because ordering a car with the desired options entailed an eight-week wait for delivery, more than 90% of customers bought their cars off the lot.

The dealer told me that he had 2 versions of the car model on his lot and that if neither matched my ideal specifications, he might be able to get my choice from another dealer in the Philadelphia area. When I got home, I checked the phone book and found ten dealers in the area. Assuming each of them also had 2 versions of the car in stock, I was choosing from a selection of at most 20 versions of a car that could be made in 20 million. In other words, the auto distribution channel is a kind of hourglass with the dealer at the neck. At the top of the glass, plants, which introduce innovations in color and technology every year, can provide an almost infinite variety of options. At the bottom, a multitude of customers with diverse tastes could benefit from that variety but are unable to because of dealers' practices at the neck of the glass.

The computer industry of 20 years ago shows that a company can supply an innovative product with an unresponsive process if the market allows it a long lead time for delivery. In my first job after college, I worked in an IBM sales office helping to market the System/360 mainframe. I was shocked to learn that IBM was then quoting a 14-month lead time for this hot new product. I asked how I could possibly tell a customer to wait that long. The answer was that if a customer really wanted a 360, it would wait, and that if I couldn't persuade it to wait, there must be something seriously lacking in my sales skills. That answer was actually correct: lead times of one to two years were then the norm. This meant that computer manufacturers had plenty of time to organize their supplies around physical efficiency.

Now PCs and workstations have replaced mainframes as the dominant technology, and the acceptable lead time has dropped to days. Yet because the industry has largely retained its emphasis on a physically efficient supply chain, most computer companies find themselves firmly positioned in the upper right-hand cell of the matrix.

That mismatch has engendered a kind of schizophrenia in the way computer companies view their supply chains. They cling to measures of physical efficiency such as plant capacity utilization and inventory turns because those measures are familiar from their mainframe days. Yet the marketplace keeps pulling them toward measures of responsiveness such as product availability.

How does a company in the upper right-hand cell overcome its schizophrenia? Either by moving to the left on the matrix and making its products functional or by moving down the matrix and making its supply chain responsive. The correct direction depends on whether the product is sufficiently innovative to generate enough additional profit to cover the cost of making the supply chain responsive.

A sure sign that a company needs to move to the left is if it has a product line characterized by frequent introductions of new offerings, great variety, and low profit margins. Toothpaste is a good example. A few years ago, I was to give a presentation to a food industry group. I decided that a good way to demonstrate the dysfunctional level of variety that exists in many grocery categories would be to buy one of each type of toothpaste made by a particular manufacturer and present the collection to my audience. When I went to my local supermarket to buy my samples, I found that 28 varieties were available. A few months later, when I mentioned this discovery to a senior vice president of a competing manufacturer, he acknowledged that his company also had 28 types of toothpaste—one to match each of the rival's offerings.

Does the world need 28 kinds of toothpaste from each manufacturer? Procter & Gamble, which has been simplifying many of its product lines and pricing, is coming to the conclusion that the answer is no. Toothpaste is a product category in which a move to the left—from innovative to functional—makes sense.

In other cases when a company has an unresponsive supply chain for innovative products, the right solution is to make some of the products functional and to create a responsive supply chain for the remaining innovative products. The automobile industry is a good example.

Many suggestions have been made for fixing the problems with the auto distribution channel I have described here, but they all miss the mark because they propose applying just one solution. This approach overlooks the fact that some cars, such as the Ford Fairmont, are inherently functional, while others, such as the BMW Z3 roadster (driven in the James Bond movie *Golden Eye*), are innovative. A lean, efficient distribution channel is exactly right for functional cars but totally inappropriate for innovative cars, which require inventory buffers to absorb uncertainty in demand. The most efficient place to put buffers is in parts, but doing so directly contradicts the just-in-time system that automakers have so vigorously adopted in the last decade. The just-in-time system has slashed parts inventories in plants (where holding inventory is relatively cheap) to a few hours, while stocks of cars at dealers (where holding inventory is expensive) have grown to around 90 days.

Efficient Supply of Functional Products

Cost reduction is familiar territory, and most companies have been at it for years. Nevertheless, there are some new twists to this old game. As companies have aggressively pursued cost cutting over the years, they have begun to reach the point of diminishing returns within their organization's own boundaries and now believe that better coordination across corporate boundaries—with suppliers and distributors—presents the greatest opportunities. Happily, the growing acceptance of this view has coincided with the emergence of electronic networks that facilitate closer coordination.

Campbell Soup has shown how this new game should be played. In 1991, the company launched the continuous-replenishment program with its most progressive retailers. The program works as follows: Campbell establishes electronic data interchange (EDI) links with retailers. Every morning, retailers electronically inform the company of their demand for all Campbell products and of the level of inventories in their distribution centers. Campbell uses that information to forecast future demand and to determine which products require replenishment based on upper and lower inventory limits previously established with each retailer. Trucks leave the Campbell shipping plant that afternoon and arrive at the retailers' distribution centers with the required replenishments the same day. The program cut the inventories of four participating retailers from about four to two weeks of supply. The company achieved this improvement because it slashed the delivery lead time and because it knows the inventories of all retailers and hence can deploy supplies of each product where they are needed the most.

Pursuing continuous replenishment made Campbell aware of the negative impact that the overuse of price promotions can have on physical efficiency. Every January, for example, there was a big spike in shipments of Chicken Noodle Soup because of deep discounts that Campbell was offering. Retailers responded to the price cut by stocking up, in some cases buying a year's

How Campbell's price promotions disrupted its supply system

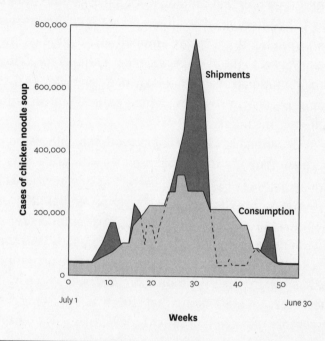

supply—a practice the industry calls *forward buying.* Nobody won on the deal. Retailers had to pay to carry the year's supply, and the shipment bulge added cost throughout the Campbell system. For example, chicken-boning plants had to go on overtime starting in October to meet the bulge. (See the exhibit "How Campbell's price promotions disrupted its supply system.") Recognizing the problem, Campbell required its retail customers on the continuous-replenishment program to waive the option of forward buying at a discounted price. A retailer that promotes Campbell products in its stores by offering a discounted price to consumers has two options: it can pay Campbell an "everyday low price" equal to the average price that a retailer receiving the promotional deals would pay or it can receive a discount on orders resulting from genuine increases in sales to consumers.

The Campbell example offers some valuable lessons. Because soup is a functional product with price-sensitive demand, Campbell was correct to pursue physical efficiency. Service—or the in-stock availability of Campbell products at a retailer's distribution center—did increase marginally, from 98.5% to 99.2%. But the big gain for the supply chain was in increased operating efficiency, through the reduction in retailers' inventories. Most retailers figure that the cost of carrying the inventory of a given product for a year equals at least 25% of what they paid for the product. A two-week inventory reduction represents a cost savings equal to nearly 1% of sales. Since the average retailer's profits equal about 2% of sales, this savings is enough to increase profits by 50%.

Because the retailer makes more money on Campbell products delivered through continuous replenishment, it has an incentive to carry a broader line of them and to give them more shelf space. For that reason, Campbell found that after it had introduced the program, sales of its products grew twice as fast through participating retailers as they did through other retailers.

Understandably, supermarket chains love programs such as Campbell's. Wegmans Food Markets, with stores in upstate New York, has even augmented its accounting system so that it can measure and reward suppliers whose products cost the least to stock and sell.

There is also an important principle about the supply of functional products lurking in the "everyday low price" feature of Campbell's program. Consumers of functional products offer companies predictable demand in exchange for a good product and a reasonable price. The challenge is to avoid actions that would destroy the inherent simplicity of this relationship. Many companies go astray because they get hooked on overusing price promotions. They start by using price incentives to pull demand forward in time to meet a quarterly revenue target. But pulling demand forward helps only once. The next quarter, a company has to pull demand forward again just to fill the hole created by the first incentive. The result is an addiction to incentives that turns simple, predictable demand into a chaotic series of spikes that only add to cost.

Finally, the Campbell story illustrates a different way for supply chain partners to interact in the pursuit of higher profits. Functional products such as groceries are usually highly price-sensitive, and negotiations along the supply chain can be fierce. If a company can get its supplier to cut its price by a penny and its customer to accept a one-cent price increase, those concessions can have a huge impact on the company's profits. In this competitive model of supply chain relations, costs in the chain are assumed to be fixed, and the manufacturer and the retailer compete through price negotiations for a bigger share of the fixed profit pie. In contrast, Campbell's continuous-replenishment program embodies a model in which the manufacturer and the retailer cooperate to cut costs throughout the chain, thereby increasing the size of the pie.

The cooperative model can be powerful, but it does have pitfalls. Too often, companies reason that there never can be too many ways to make money, and they decide to play the cooperative and competitive games at the same time. But that tactic doesn't work, because the two approaches require diametrically different behavior. For example, consider information sharing. If you are my supplier and we are negotiating over price, the last thing you want to do is fully share with me information about your costs. But that is what we both must do if we want to reduce supply chain costs by assigning each task to whichever of us can perform it most cheaply.

Responsive Supply of Innovative Products

Uncertainty about demand is intrinsic to innovative products. As a result, figuring out how to cope with it is the primary challenge in creating a responsive supply process for such products. I have seen companies use four tools to cope with uncertainty in demand. To fashion a responsive supply process, managers need to understand each of them and then blend them in a recipe that's right for their company's particular situation.

Although it may sound obvious, the first step for many companies is simply to *accept* that uncertainty is inherent in innovative products. Companies that grew up in an oligopoly with less competition, more docile customers, and weaker retailers find it difficult to accept the high levels of demand uncertainty that exist today in many markets. They have a tendency to declare a high level of forecast errors unacceptable, and they virtually command their people to think hard enough and long enough to achieve accuracy in their forecasts. But these companies can't remove uncertainty by decree. When it comes to innovative products, uncertainty must be accepted as good. If the demand for a product were predictable, that product probably would not be sufficiently innovative to command high profit margins. The fact is that risk and return are linked, and the highest profit margins usually go with the highest risk in demand.

Once a company has accepted the uncertainty of demand, it can employ three coordinated strategies to manage that uncertainty. It can continue to strive to *reduce* uncertainty—for example, by finding sources of new data that can serve as leading indicators or by having different products share common components as much as possible so that the demand for components becomes more predictable. It can *avoid* uncertainty by cutting lead times and increasing the supply chain's flexibility so that it can produce to order or at least manufacture the product at a time closer to when demand materializes and can be accurately forecast. Finally, once uncertainty has been reduced or avoided as much as possible, it can *hedge against* the remaining residual uncertainty with buffers of inventory or excess capacity.

The experiences of National Bicycle, a subsidiary of Matsushita Electric, and of Sport Obermeyer illustrate the different ways in which these three strategies can be blended to create a responsive supply chain.

National Bicycle prospered for decades as a small but successful division. But by the mid-1980s, it was in trouble. Bicycles in Japan were functional products bought mainly as an inexpensive means of transportation, and sales were flat. Bicycles had become a commodity sold on the basis of low price, and Japan's high labor costs left National Bicycle unable to compete with inexpensive bikes from Taiwan and Korea.

In 1986, in an attempt to salvage the situation, Matsushita appointed as president of National an executive from another division who had no experience in bicycles. The new president, Makoto Komoto, saw that the division had many strengths: technical expertise in manufacturing and computers, a highly skilled workforce, a strong brand name (Panasonic), and a network of 9,000 dealers. Komoto also noticed that National Bicycle had an innovative product segment that enjoyed high profit margins: sports bicycles that affluent customers bought purely for recreation. He concluded that National's only hope was to focus on that segment and use the division's strengths to develop a responsive chain that could supply sports bikes while avoiding the high risk of overproduction that resulted from their short life cycle and uncertain demand.

According to Komoto's vision, a customer would visit a Panasonic dealership and choose a bike from a selection of 2 million options for combining size, color, and components, using a special measuring stand to find the exact size of the frame that he or she needed. The order would be faxed to the factory, where computer-controlled welding equipment and skilled workers would make the bike and deliver it to the customer within two weeks.

Komoto's radical vision became a reality in 1987. By 1991, fueled by this innovation, National Bicycle had increased its share of the sports bicycle market in Japan from 5% to 29%. It was meeting the two-week lead time 99.99% of the time and was in the black.

National Bicycle's success is a good example of a responsive supply chain achieved through avoiding uncertainty. National has little idea what customers will order when they walk into a retail shop, but that doesn't matter: its produce-to-order system allows it to match supply with demand as it happens. By radically increasing the number of choices from a few types of bikes to 2 million, it can induce the customer to sacrifice immediate availability and wait two weeks for a bicycle.

National's program is part of a new movement called *mass customization:* building the ability to customize a large volume of products and deliver them at close to mass-production prices. Many other companies have found that they, too, can benefit from this strategy. For example, Lutron Electronics of Coopersburg, Pennsylvania, became the world leader in dimmer switches and other lighting controls by giving customers an essentially unlimited choice of technical and fashion features. Says Michael W. Pessina, Lutron's vice president of manufacturing operations, "With our diverse product line, customer demand can be impossible to predict. Yet by configuring products at the time of order, we can offer customers tremendous variety and fill orders very quickly without having to stock a huge amount of inventory."

Mass customization is not without its challenges. For example, what does National Bicycle do with its plant during the winter, when no one is buying bikes? It builds an inventory of high-end sports bicycles. In addition, mass customization is not necessarily cheap. National's custom production requires three times more labor than assembly-line mass production of bikes. Interestingly, one of the main reasons why Henry Ford in the early 1900s moved in the opposite direction—from craft to mass production—was to slash labor costs, which he succeeded in doing by a factor of three. So what has changed to make custom production viable now? Affluent consumers are willing to pay for high-margin, innovative products; and those products require a different, more expensive, but more responsive production process than the functional Model T did.

Sport Obermeyer, which is based in Aspen, Colorado, designs and manufactures fashion skiwear and distributes it through 800 specialty retailers located throughout the United States. Because 95% of its products are new each year, it constantly faces the challenges and risks of demand uncertainty: stockouts of hot styles during the selling season and leftover inventory of "dogs" at the end of the season. In 1991, the company's vice president, Walter R. Obermeyer, launched a project to attack those problems by blending the three strategies of reducing, avoiding, and hedging against uncertainty. To reduce uncertainty, Sport Obermeyer solicited early orders from important customers: the company invited its 25 largest retailers to Aspen each February to evaluate its new line. Sport Obermeyer found that the early orders from this handful of retailers permitted it to forecast national demand for all its products with a margin of error of just 10%.

Although it was helpful to get this information several months before Sport Obermeyer was required to ship its products in September, it didn't solve the company's problem, because long lead times forced it to commit itself to products well before February. Obermeyer concluded that each day shaved off the lead time would save the company $25,000 because that was the amount it spent each day at the end of September shipping products by air from plants in Asia to have them in stores by early October—the start of the retail season. Once that figure was announced to employees, they found all kinds of ways to shorten the lead time. For example, the person who had dutifully used standard mail service to get design information to the production manager in Hong Kong realized that the $25 express-mail charge was a bargain compared with the $25,000 per day in added costs resulting from longer lead times caused by mail delays. Through such efforts, Sport Obermeyer was able to avoid uncertainty on half of its production by committing that production after early orders had been received in February.

Nevertheless, the company still had to commit half of the production early in the season, when demand was uncertain. Which styles should it make then? It would stand to reason that they should be the styles for which Sport Obermeyer had the most confidence in its forecasts. But how could it tell which those were? Then the company noticed something interesting. Obermeyer had asked each of the six members of a committee responsible for forecasting to construct a forecast for all products, and he used the average of the six forecasts as the company's forecast. After one year of trying this method, the company found that when the six individual forecasts agreed, the average was accurate, and when they disagreed, the average was inaccurate. This discovery gave Sport Obermeyer a means of selecting the styles to make early. Using this information as well as data on the cost of overproduction and underproduction, it developed a model for hedging against the risk of both problems. The model tells the company exactly how much of each style to make early in the production season (which begins nearly a year before the retail season) and how much to make in February, after early orders are received.

Sport Obermeyer's approach, which has been called *accurate response,* has cut the cost of both overproduction and underproduction in half—enough to increase profits by 60%. And retailers love the fact that the system results in more than 99% product availability: they have ranked Sport Obermeyer number one in the industry for service. (See "Making Supply Meet Demand in an Uncertain World," by Marshall L. Fisher, Janice H. Hammond, Walter R. Obermeyer, and Ananth Raman, HBR May-June 1994.)

Companies such as Sport Obermeyer, National Bicycle, and Campbell Soup, however, are still the exceptions. Managers at many companies continue to lament that although they know their supply chains are riddled with waste and generate great dissatisfaction among customers, they don't know what to do about the problem. The root cause could very well be a misalignment of their supply and product strategies. Realigning the two is hardly easy. But the reward—a remarkable competitive advantage that generates high growth in sales and profits—makes the effort worth it.

Note

1. The contribution margin equals price minus variable cost divided by price and is expressed as a percentage. This type of profit margin measures increases in profits produced by the incremental sales that result from fewer stockouts. Consequently, it is a good way to track improvements in inventory management.

MARSHALL L. FISHER is the Stephen J. Heyman Professor of Operations and Information Management at the University of Pennsylvania's Wharton School.

Originally published in March 1997. Reprint 8509

We're in This Together

by Douglas M. Lambert and A. Michael Knemeyer

WHEN MANAGERS FROM WENDY'S International and Tyson Foods sat down together in December 2003 to craft a supply chain partnership, each side arrived at the table with misgivings. There were those on the Wendy's side who remembered all too well the disagreements they'd had with Tyson in the past. In fact, just a few years earlier, Wendy's had made a formal decision not to buy from Tyson again. On the Tyson side, some people were wary of a customer whose demands had prevented the business from meeting its profit goals.

A few things had changed in the meantime, or the companies wouldn't have been at the table at all. First, the menu at Wendy's had shifted with consumer tastes—chicken had become just as important as beef. The restaurant chain had a large-volume chicken supplier, but it wanted to find yet another. Second, Tyson had acquired leading beef supplier IBP, with which Wendy's had a strong relationship. IBP's president and

COO, Richard Bond, now held the positions of president and COO of the combined organization, so Wendy's felt it had someone it could work with at Tyson.

One other thing had changed, too. The companies had a new tool, called the partnership model, to help start the relationship off on the right foot. Developed under the auspices of Ohio State University's Global Supply Chain Forum, the model incorporated lessons learned from the best partnering experiences of that group's 15 member companies. It offered a process for aligning expectations and determining the level of cooperation that would be most productive.

With this article, we put that tool in your hands. We'll explain how, over the course of a day and a half, it illuminates the drivers behind each company's desire for partnership, allows managers to examine the conditions that facilitate or hamper cooperation, and specifies which activities managers in the two companies must perform, and at what level, to implement the partnership. The model—proven at Wendy's and in dozens of other partnership efforts—rapidly establishes the mutual understanding and commitment required for success and provides a structure for measuring outcomes.

No Partnership for Its Own Sake

Why do so many partnerships fail to deliver value? Often it's because they shouldn't have existed in the first place. Partnerships are costly to implement—they require extra communication, coordination, and risk sharing. They are justified only if they stand to yield

Idea in Brief

When managers from Wendy's International and Tyson Foods got together in 2003 to craft a supply chain partnership, each side had misgivings. There were those in the Wendy's camp who remembered past disagreements with Tyson and those on the Tyson side who were wary of Wendy's. But the companies had a tool, called the "partnership model," to help get things started on the right foot. Drawing on the experiences of member companies of the Global Supply Chain Forum at Ohio State University, the model offers a process for aligning expectations and determining the most productive level of partnering. It rapidly establishes the mutual understanding and commitment required for success and provides a structure for measuring outcomes. This article puts the tool in the reader's hands. Partnerships are justified only if they stand to yield substantially better results than the firms could achieve on their own. And even if they are warranted, they can fail if the partners enter them with mismatched expectations. Over the course of a day and a half, the partnership model elucidates the drivers behind each company's desire for partnership, allows managers to examine the conditions that facilitate or hamper cooperation, and specifies which activities managers must perform to implement the relationship. This tool has proved effective at Wendy's and elsewhere in determining what type of partnership is most appropriate. Colgate-Palmolive, for example, used it to help achieve stretch financial goals with suppliers of innovative products. But the model is just as effective in revealing that some companies' visions of partnership are not justified. In matters of the heart, it may be better to have loved and lost, but in business relationships, it's better to have headed off the resource sink and lingering resentments a failed partnership can cause.

substantially better results than the firms could achieve without partnering.

This point was driven home for us early in our research with the Global Supply Chain Forum when its members identified successful partnerships for study. One was an arrangement between a package delivery company and a manufacturer. The delivery company got the revenue it had been promised, and the manufacturer got the cost and service levels that had been stipulated. But it wasn't a partnership; it was a single-source contract with volume guaranteed. The point is that it's often possible to get the results you want without a partnership. If that's the case, don't create one. Just write a good contract. You simply don't have enough human resources to form tight relationships with every supplier or customer.

At Wendy's, managers distinguish between high- and low-value partnership opportunities using a two-by-two matrix with axes labeled "complexity to Wendy's" and "volume of the buy." Supplies such as drinking straws might be purchased in huge volumes, but they present no complexities in terms of taste, texture, or safety. Only if both volume and complexity are high—as with key ingredients—does Wendy's seek a partnership. Colgate-Palmolive similarly plots suppliers on a matrix according to "potential for cost reductions" and "potential for innovation" and explores partnering opportunities with those that rank high in both.

Reserving partnerships for situations where they're justified is one way to ensure they deliver value. Even then, however, they can fail if partners enter into them with mismatched expectations. Like the word "commitment" in a marriage, "partnership" can be interpreted quite differently by the parties involved—and both sides often are so certain that their interpretations are shared that their assumptions are never articulated or questioned.

What's needed, then, for supply chain partnerships to succeed is a way of targeting high-potential relationships and aligning expectations around them. This is what the partnership model is designed to do. It is not designed to be a supplier-selection tool. At Wendy's, for instance, the model was employed only after the company's senior vice president of supply chain management, Judy Hollis, had reduced the company's supplier base, consolidating to 225 suppliers. At that point, Wendy's could say: "Now the decision's been made. You're a supplier. Your business isn't at risk. What we're trying to do here is structure the relationship so we get the most out of it for the least amount of effort." That assurance helped people to speak more frankly about their hopes for the partnership—an absolute necessity for the partnership-building process to succeed.

A Forum for Frank Discussion

Under the model, key representatives of two potential partners come together for a day and a half to focus solely on the partnership. Little preparatory work is required of them, but the same can't be said for the meeting's organizers (usually staff people from the company that has initiated the process). The organizers face a number of important tasks before the session. First, they must find a suitable location, preferably off-site for both parties. Second, they must engage a session leader. It doesn't work to have someone who is associated with one of the companies, as we know from the experience of forum members. We recall one session in

The Partnership Model

WHEN THE MEMBER COMPANIES of the Global Supply Chain Forum first convened in 1992, they agreed they needed insights on how to build effective partnerships. Research on their experiences formed the basis of a model that has been refined through dozens of partnership facilitation sessions. Managers state the drivers behind their desire to partner and examine the conditions that would facilitate cooperation. The model helps them decide on a partnership type and boost the needed managerial components. Later, if the partners aren't happy with the relationship, they determine whether drivers or facilitators have changed or components are at an appropriate level.

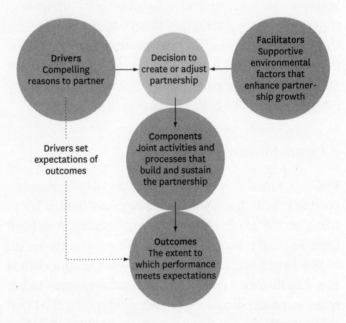

Diagram source: Douglas M. Lambert, Margaret A. Emmelhainz, and John T. Gardner, "So You Think You Want a Partner?" *Marketing Management*, Summer 1996.

particular run by Don Jablonski of Masterfoods USA's purchasing operation. Don is an all-around good guy, is very able at running sessions, and was familiar with the model, but the supplier's people clammed up and the session went nowhere. They needed an outsider.

Third, the organizers must do some calendar juggling to ensure that the right people attend on both sides. Though there is no magic number of representatives, each team should include a broad mix of managers and individuals with functional expertise. The presence of high-level executives ensures that the work won't be second-guessed, and middle managers, operations people, and staff personnel from departments such as HR, finance, and marketing can provide valuable perspectives on the companies' expected day-to-day interactions.

Goals in the Cold Light of Day

After introductions and an overview, the morning of the first day is consumed by the "drivers session," in which each side's team considers a potential partnership in terms of "What's in it for us?" (See the sidebar "How to Commit in 28 Hours.")

The teams are separated in two rooms, and each is asked to discuss and then list the compelling reasons, from its point of view, for a partnership. It's vital that participants feel free to speak frankly about whether and how their own company could benefit from such a relationship. What are the potential payoffs? For some teams, there aren't many. Other teams fill page after page of flip charts.

How to Commit in 28 Hours

Before the Meeting

A cross-functional, multilevel team from each company is identified and commits to a meeting time. A location is found, preferably off-site for both parties.

Day One
Morning

Introductions and an Overview. The session leader explains the rationale for using the model.

Articulation of Drivers. The two teams meet separately to discuss why they are seeking a partnership and to list specific, selfish reasons in four categories: asset and cost efficiencies, customer service improvements, marketing advantages, and profit growth or stability. A score is assigned to each category, indicating the likelihood that the partnership would serve those goals.

Afternoon

Presentation of Drivers. The groups present their drivers to each other. Each team must challenge every driver it considers unsupportable or unacceptable. Failure to challenge a goal implies agreement and obligates the organization to help the potential partner achieve the aim. The teams also compare driver scores.

The partnership drivers fall into four categories—asset and cost efficiencies, customer service enhancements, marketing advantages, and profit growth or stability. The session leader and the provided forms ensure that each of these categories is explicitly addressed. For example, under asset and cost efficiencies, a team might specify desired savings in product costs, distribution, packaging, or information handling. The goal is for the participants to build specific bullet-point descriptions for each driver

The lower of the two becomes the driver score for the proposed partnership (that's because the less motivated team is the relationship's limiting factor).

Evaluation of Facilitators. The teams jointly examine the features of the shared organizational environment that would help or hinder cooperation. Scores are assigned to four basic and five additional factors.

Prescription of Partnership Level. The group consults the propensity-to-partner matrix, which yields a prescription based on the scores. The ideal relationship looks like a Type I, II, or III partnership or simply an arm's-length association.

Day Two
Morning

Examination of Components. The group examines the management components required for the level of partnership prescribed by the matrix and considers to what extent those components currently exist on both sides. A plan is made for developing needed components. The plans include specific actions, responsible parties, and due dates.

Review. The drivers articulated on day one are reviewed to ensure that each has been targeted with specific action plans.

---

category with metrics and targets. For the session leader, whose job is to get the teams to articulate measurable goals, this may be the toughest part of the day. It isn't enough for a team to say that the company is looking for "improved asset utilization" or "product cost savings." The goals must be specific, such as improving utilization from 80% to 98% or cutting product costs by 7% per year.

Next, the teams use a five-point scale (1 being "no chance" and 5 being "certain") to rate the likelihood that the partnership will deliver the desired results in each of the four major categories. An extra point is awarded (raising the score to as high as 6) if the result would yield a sustainable competitive advantage by matching or exceeding the industry benchmark in that area. The scores are added (the highest possible score is 24) to produce a total driver score for each side.

This is the point at which the day gets interesting. The teams reassemble in one room and present their drivers and scores to each other. The rules of the game are made clear. If one side doesn't understand how the other's goals would be met, it must push for clarification. Failure to challenge a driver implies agreement and obligates the partners to cooperate on it. The drivers listed by a Wendy's supplier, for instance, included the prospect of doing more business with the Canadian subsidiary of Wendy's, Tim Hortons. The Wendy's team rejected the driver, explaining that the subsidiary's management made decisions autonomously. This is just the sort of expectation that is left unstated in most partnerships and later becomes a source of disappointment.

But expectations are adjusted upward as often as they are lowered. On several occasions, managers reacting to a drivers presentation have been pleasantly surprised to discover a shared goal that hadn't been raised earlier because both sides had assumed it wouldn't fly with the other.

The drivers session is invaluable in getting everyone's motivations onto the table and calibrating the two sides' expectations. It also offers a legitimate forum for discussing contentious issues or clearing the air on past grievances. During one Wendy's session, the discussion veered off on a very useful tangent about why the company's specifications were costly to meet. In another memorable session, we heard a manager on the buying side of a relationship say, "I feel like this is a marriage that's reached the point where you don't think I'm as beautiful as I used to be." His counterpart snapped: "Well, maybe you're not the woman I married anymore." The candor of the subsequent discussion allowed the two sides to refocus on what they could gain by working together. As Judy Hollis told us about the Wendy's-Tyson session, "What they presented to us during the sharing of drivers confirmed that we could have a deeper relationship with them. If we had seen things that were there just to please us, we wouldn't have been willing to go forward with a deeper relationship."

The Search for Compatibility

Once the two sides have reached agreement on the business results they hope to achieve, the focus shifts to the organizational environment in which the partnership would function. In a new session, the two sides jointly consider the extent to which they believe certain key factors that we call "facilitators" are in place to support the venture. The four most important are compatibility of corporate cultures, compatibility of management philosophy and techniques, a strong sense of mutuality, and symmetry between the two parties. The group, as a whole, is asked to score—again, on a five-point scale—the facilitators' perceived strengths. (This implies, of course, that the participants have a history of interaction on which to draw. If the relationship is new, managers will need to spend some time working on joint projects before they can attempt this assessment.)

For culture and for management philosophy and techniques, the point is not to look for sameness. Partners needn't have identical cultures or management approaches; some differences are benign. Instead, participants are asked to consider differences that are bound to create problems. Does one company's management push decision making down into the organization while the other's executives issue orders from on high? Is one side committed to continuous improvement and the other not? Are people compensated in conflicting ways? The session leader must counter the groups' natural tendency to paint too rosy a picture of how well the organizations would mesh. He or she can accomplish this by asking for an example to illustrate any cultural or management similarity participants may cite. Once the example is on the table, someone in the room will often counter it by saying, "Yeah, but they also do *this* . . ."

A sense of mutuality—of shared purpose and perspective—is vital. It helps the organizations move beyond a zero-sum mentality and respect the spirit of partnership, even if the earnings of one partner are under pressure. It may extend to a willingness to integrate systems or share certain financial information. Symmetry often means comparable scale, industry position, or brand image. But even if two companies are quite dissimilar in these respects, they might assign themselves a high score on symmetry if they hold equal power over each other's marketplace success—perhaps because the smaller company supplies a component that is unique, in scarce supply, or critical to the larger company's competitive advantage.

Beyond these four major facilitators, five others remain to be assessed: shared competitors, physical proximity, potential for exclusivity, prior relationship experience, and shared end users. Each can add one point to the total, for a maximum facilitator score of 25. These factors won't cripple a partnership if they are absent, but where they are present, they deepen the connection. Think of the extra closeness it must have given the McDonald's and Coke partnership in the 1990s that both companies loved to hate Pepsi (which at the time owned Kentucky Fried Chicken, Taco Bell, and Pizza Hut franchises, giving it more locations than McDonald's). Physical proximity certainly adds a dimension to the partnership Wendy's has with sauce supplier T. Marzetti. With both headquarters in Columbus, Ohio, the two companies' R&D staffs can collaborate easily. We saw the benefits of proximity, too, in 3M and Target's partnership. Twin Cities–based managers accustomed to interacting through local charities, arts organizations, and community-building efforts found it easy to collaborate in their work.

Assessing these issues carefully and accurately is worth the sometimes considerable effort, because the scores on facilitators and on drivers in the first session yield a prescription for partnering. The exhibit

The propensity-to-partner matrix

What type of partnership would be best? Once they have measured their desire to partner and determined how easily they could coordinate activities, companies considering working together can use this matrix to decide whether to form a partnership and, if so, at what level.

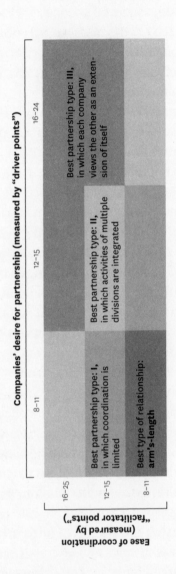

Companies' desire for partnership (measured by "driver points")

	8–11	12–15	16–24
16–25			Best partnership type: **III**, in which each company views the other as an extension of itself
12–15		Best partnership type: **II**, in which activities of multiple divisions are integrated	
8–11	Best partnership type: **I**, in which coordination is limited		

Ease of coordination (measured by "facilitator points")

Best type of relationship: arm's-length

"The propensity-to-partner matrix" shows how the scores indicate which type of association would be best—a Type I, II, or III partnership or simply an arm's-length relationship. The types entail varying levels of managerial complexity and resource use. In Type I, the organizations recognize each other as partners and co-ordinate activities and planning on a limited basis. In Type II, the companies integrate activities involving multiple divisions and functions. In Type III, they share a significant level of integration, with each viewing the other as an extension of itself. Type III partnerships are equivalent, in alliance terminology, to strategic alliances, but we are careful to avoid such value-laden language because there should be no implication that more integration is better than less integration.

To put this in perspective, recall that Wendy's began by consolidating its buying to 225 suppliers. Of these, only the top 40 are being taken through the partner-ship-model process. And it appears that only a few of the partnerships will end up being Type III. Perhaps 12 or 15 will be Type II, and about 20 will be Type I. This feels like an appropriate distribution. We don't want participants aspiring to Type III partnerships. We sim-ply want them to fit the type of relationship to the busi-ness situation and the organizational environment.

Naturally, the managers in the room do not have to simply accept the prescription. If the outcome surprises them in any way, it may well be time for a reality check. They should ask themselves: "Is it reasonable to com-mit the resources for this type of partnership, given what we know of our drivers and the facilitators?" If the answer is in doubt, the final session of the process, focusing on the managerial requirements of the partnership, will clarify matters.

Action Items and Time Frames

In the third session, the group reconvenes as a whole to focus on management components—the joint activities and processes required to launch and sustain the partnership. While drivers and facilitators determine which type of relationship would be best, management components are the building blocks of partnership. They include capabilities for planning, joint operating controls, communication, and risk/reward sharing. They are universal across firms and across business environments and, unlike drivers and facilitators, are under the direct control of the managers involved.

The two teams jointly develop action plans to put these components in place at a level that is appropriate for the partnership type. Participants are provided with a table of components, listed in order of importance (a portion of such a table is shown in the exhibit "Management components for partnerships"). The first task is for the teams to determine the degree to which the components are already in place. This is a quick process; the participants run through the components in the table, noting whether each type of activity is performed at a high, medium, or low level. Generally speaking, the components should be at a high level for Type III partnerships, a medium level for Type II, and a low level for Type I.

Under the heading of joint operating controls, for example, a Type III partnership would call for developing performance measures jointly and focusing those measures on the companies' combined performance. A Type II partnership, by contrast, would involve performance measures that focus on each company's individual performance, regardless of how well the partner performs. In a Type I partnership, the companies would not work together to develop mutually satisfactory performance measures, though they might share their results.

For each management component, the group must outline what, if anything, needs to be done to move from the current state to the capability level required by the partnership. Here, it is helpful to refocus on the drivers agreed to in session one and start developing action plans around each of them. It is in these action plans that the deficiencies of the current management components become apparent. It may be, for instance, that achieving a particular goal depends on systematic joint planning, but the group has just said planning is being performed at a low level. Clearly, planning must be ratcheted up.

One of the needs that became clear in the Tyson-Wendy's session was for increased communication at the upper levels. People at the operational level in the two companies were communicating regularly and effectively, but there was no parallel for that at the top. Joe Gordon, a commodity manager at Wendy's, explained why this was a problem: "All of us worker bees sometimes come to a point where we have obstacles in

Management components for partnerships*

Partnership component	Low	Medium	High
Planning: Style	▪ on ad hoc basis	▪ regularly scheduled	▪ systematic: both scheduled and ad hoc
▪ Level	▪ focus is on projects or tasks	▪ focus is on process	▪ focus is on relationship
▪ Content	▪ sharing of existing plans	▪ performed jointly, eliminating conflicts in strategies	▪ performed jointly and at multiple levels, including top management; each party participates in other's business planning
Joint operating controls: Measurement	▪ performance measures are developed independently, but results might be shared	▪ measures are jointly developed and shared; focus is on individual firms' performance	▪ measures are jointly developed and shared; focus is on relationship and joint performance
▪ Ability to make changes	▪ parties may suggest changes to other's system	▪ parties may make changes to other's system after getting approval	▪ parties may make changes to other's system without getting approval

Component			
Communication:			
NONROUTINE	• very limited, usually just critical issues at the task or project level	• conducted more regularly, done at multiple levels; generally open and honest	• planned as part of the relationship; occurs at all levels; sharing of praise and criticism; parties "speak the same language"
DAY-TO-DAY			
• Organization	• conducted on ad hoc basis, between individuals	• limited number of scheduled communications; some routinization	• systematized method of communication; communication systems are linked
• Balance	• primarily one-way	• two-way but unbalanced	• balanced two-way communication flow
• Electronic	• use of individual systems	• joint modification of individual systems	• joint development of customized electronic communications
Risk/reward/sharing:			
• Loss tolerance	• very low tolerance for loss	• some tolerance for short-term loss	• high tolerance for short-term loss
• Gain commitment	• limited willingness to help the other gain	• willingness to help the other gain	• desire to help other party gain
• Commitment to fairness	• fairness is evaluated by transaction	• fairness is tracked year to year	• fairness is measured over life of relationship

*In general, Type III partnerships require high levels of most of these components, Type II partnerships require medium levels, and Type I relationships require low levels. (This is just a partial list of managerial components.)

our day-to-day relationship, and in the past we might have given up on trying to overcome them." After an action plan was outlined for getting the top management teams together to talk, those problems became easier to address.

When the participants leave, they leave with action items, time frames for carrying them out, and a designation of responsible parties. The fact that so much is accomplished in such a brief period is a source of continued motivation. Donnie King, who heads Tyson's poultry operations, admitted that he had been skeptical going into the meeting. "You tend to believe it is going to be a process where you sit around the campfire and hold hands and sing 'Kumbaya' and nothing changes," he said. But when he left the meeting, he knew there would be change indeed.

A Versatile Tool

The current quality of interaction and cooperation between Tyson Foods and Wendy's International suggests that the partnership model is effective not only in designing new relationships but also in turning around troubled ones. Today, Wendy's buys heavily from Tyson and believes the partnership produces value similar to that of the other Wendy's key-ingredient partnerships. Richard Bond of Tyson told us: "There is a greater level of trust between the two companies. We have had a higher level of involvement in QA regulations and how our plants are audited [by Wendy's], rather than having [those processes] dictated to us."

The two companies' R&D and marketing groups have begun to explore new products that would allow Wendy's to expand its menu, with Tyson as a key supplier. In a recent interview, we asked the director of supply chain management for Wendy's, Tony Scherer, to recall the tense conversations of the December 2003 partnership session, and we wondered whether that history still colored the relationship. "No," he said. "I really do feel like we've dropped it now, and we can move on."

For other companies, the partnership model has paid off in different ways. Colgate-Palmolive used it to help achieve stretch financial goals with key suppliers of innovative products. TaylorMade-adidas Golf Company used it to structure supplier relationships in China. At International Paper, the model helped to align expectations between two divisions that supply each other and have distinct P&Ls. And it served Cargill well when the company wanted several of its divisions, all dealing separately with Masterfoods USA, to present a more unified face to the customer. The session was unwieldy, with seven Cargill groups interacting with three Masterfoods divisions, but the give-and-take yielded a wide range of benefits, from better utilization of a Cargill cocoa plant in Brazil to more effective hedging of commodity price risk at Masterfoods.

But to focus only on these success stories is to miss much of the point of the model. Just as valuable, we would argue, are the sessions in which participants discover that their vision of partnership is not justified by the benefits it can reasonably be expected to yield. In matters of the heart, it may be better to have loved and lost, but in business relationships, it's far better to have avoided the resource sink and lingering resentments of a failed partnership. Study the relationships that have ended up as disappointments to one party or both, and you will find a common theme: mismatched and unrealistic expectations. Executives in each firm were using the same word, "partnership," but envisioning different relationships. The partnership model ensures that both parties see the opportunity wholly and only for what it is.

DOUGLAS M. LAMBERT holds the Raymond E. Mason Chair in Transportation and Logistics and **A. MICHAEL KNEMEYER** is an assistant professor of logistics at the Ohio State University's Fisher College of Business.

Originally published in December 2004. Reprint R0412H

Rapid-Fire Fulfillment

by Kasra Ferdows, Michael A. Lewis, and Jose A.D. Machuca

WHEN A GERMAN WHOLESALER suddenly canceled a big lingerie order in 1975, Amancio Ortega thought his fledgling clothing company might go bankrupt. All his capital was tied up in the order. There were no other buyers. In desperation, he opened a shop near his factory in La Coruña, in the far northwest corner of Spain, and sold the goods himself. He called the shop Zara.

Today, over 650 Zara stores in some 50 countries attract well-heeled customers in luxury shopping districts around the world, and Senor Ortega is arguably the richest man in Spain. The clothing company he founded, called Inditex, has been growing ever since he opened that first Zara shop. From 1991 to 2003, Inditex's sales—70% of which spring from Zara—grew more than 12-fold from €367 million to €4.6 billion, and net profits ballooned 14-fold from €31 million to €447 million. In May 2001, a particularly tough period for initial public offerings, Inditex sold 25% of its shares to the public for

€2.3 billion. While many of its competitors have exhibited poor financial results over the last three years, Zara's sales and net income have continued to grow at an annual rate of over 20%.

The lesson Ortega learned from his early scare was this: To be successful, "you need to have five fingers touching the factory and five touching the customer." Translation: Control what happens to your product until the customer buys it. In adhering to this philosophy, Zara has developed a superresponsive supply chain. The company can design, produce, and deliver a new garment and put it on display in its stores worldwide in a mere 15 days. Such a pace is unheard-of in the fashion business, where designers typically spend months planning for the next season. Because Zara can offer a large variety of the latest designs quickly and in limited quantities, it collects 85% of the full ticket price on its retail clothing, while the industry average is 60% to 70%. As a result, it achieves a higher net margin on sales than its competitors; in 2001, for example, when Inditex's net margin was 10.5%, Benetton's was only 7%, H&M's was 9.5%, and Gap's was near zero.

Zara defies most of the current conventional wisdom about how supply chains should be run. In fact, some of Zara's practices may seem questionable, if not downright crazy, when taken individually. Unlike so many of its peers in retail clothing that rush to outsource, Zara keeps almost half of its production in-house. Far from pushing its factories to maximize their output, the company intentionally leaves extra capacity. Rather than chase economies of scale, Zara manufactures and dis-

Idea in Brief

Would you send a half-empty truck across Europe or pay to airfreight coats to Japan twice a week? Would you move unsold items out of your shop after only two weeks? Would you run your factories just during the day shift? Is this any way to run an efficient supply chain? For Spanish clothier Zara it is. Not that any one of these tactics is especially effective in itself. Rather, they stem from a holistic approach to supply chain management that optimizes the entire chain instead of focusing on individual parts. In the process, Zara defies most of the current conventional wisdom about how supply chains should be run. Unlike so many of its peers, which rush to outsource, Zara keeps almost half of its production in-house. Far from pushing its factories to maximize output, the company focuses capital on building extra capacity. Rather than chase economies of scale, Zara manufactures and distributes

products in small batches. Instead of outside partners, the company manages all design, warehousing, distribution, and logistics functions itself. The result is a superresponsive supply chain exquisitely tailored to Zara's business model. Zara can design, produce, and deliver a new garment to its 600-plus stores worldwide in a mere 15 days. So in Zara's shops, customers can always find new products—but in limited supply. Customers think, "This green shirt fits me, and there is one on the rack. If I don't buy it now, I'll lose my chance." That urgency translates into high profit margins and steady 20% yearly growth in a tough economic climate. Some of Zara's specific practices may be directly applicable only in industries where product life cycles are very short. But Zara's simple philosophy of reaping bottom-line profits through end-to-end control of the supply chain can be applied to any industry.

tributes products in small batches. Instead of relying on outside partners, the company manages all design, warehousing, distribution, and logistics functions itself. Even many of its day-to-day operational procedures differ from the norm. It holds its retail stores to a rigid timetable for placing orders and receiving stock. It puts price tags on items before they're shipped, rather than at each store. It leaves large areas empty in its expensive retail shops. And it tolerates, even encourages, occasional stock-outs.

During the last three years, we've tried to discover just how Zara designs and manages its rapid-fire supply chain. We conducted a series of interviews with senior managers at Inditex and examined company documents and a wide range of other sources. We were particularly curious to see if Zara had discovered any groundbreaking innovations. We didn't find any. Instead, we found a self-reinforcing system built on three principles:

- **Close the communication loop.** Zara's supply chain is organized to transfer both hard data and anecdotal information quickly and easily from shoppers to designers and production staff. It's also set up to track materials and products in real time every step of the way, including inventory on display in the stores. The goal is to close the information loop between the end users and the upstream operations of design, procurement, production, and distribution as quickly and directly as possible.

- **Stick to a rhythm across the entire chain.** At Zara, rapid timing and synchronicity are paramount. To this end, the company indulges in an approach that can best be characterized as "penny foolish, pound wise." It spends money on anything that helps to increase and enforce the speed and responsiveness of the chain as a whole.

- **Leverage your capital assets to increase supply chain flexibility.** Zara has made major capital investments in production and distribution facilities and uses them to increase the supply chain's responsiveness to new and fluctuating demands. It produces complicated products in-house and outsources the simple ones.

It took Zara many years to develop its highly responsive system, but your company need not spend decades bringing its supply chain up to speed. Instead, you can borrow a page from Zara's playbook. Some of Zara's practices may be directly applicable only in high-tech or other industries where product life cycles are very short. But Ortega's simple philosophy of reaping profits through end-to-end control of the supply chain applies to any industry—from paper to aluminum products to medical instruments. Zara shows managers not only how to adjust to quixotic consumer demands but also how to resist management fads and ever-shifting industry practices.

Close the Loop

In Zara stores, customers can always find new products—but they're in limited supply. There is a sense of tantalizing exclusivity, since only a few items are on display even though stores are spacious (the average size is around 1,000 square meters). A customer thinks, "This green shirt fits me, and there is one on the rack. If I don't buy it now, I'll lose my chance."

Such a retail concept depends on the regular creation and rapid replenishment of small batches of new goods. Zara's designers create approximately 40,000 new designs annually, from which 10,000 are selected for production. Some of them resemble the latest couture creations. But Zara often beats the high-fashion houses to the market and offers almost the same products, made with less expensive fabric, at much lower prices. Since most garments come in five to six colors and five to seven sizes, Zara's system has to deal with something in the realm of 300,000 new stock-keeping units (SKUs), on average, every year.

This "fast fashion" system depends on a constant exchange of information throughout every part of Zara's supply chain—from customers to store managers, from store managers to market specialists and designers, from designers to production staff, from buyers to subcontractors, from warehouse managers to distributors, and so on. Most companies insert layers of bureaucracy that can bog down communication between departments. But Zara's organization, operational procedures, performance measures, and even its office layouts are all designed to make information transfer easy.

Zara's single, centralized design and production center is attached to Inditex headquarters in La Coruña. It consists of three spacious halls—one for women's clothing lines, one for men's, and one for children's. Unlike most companies, which try to excise redundant labor to cut costs, Zara makes a point of running three parallel, but operationally distinct, product families. Accordingly, separate design, sales, and procurement and production-planning staffs are dedicated to each clothing line. A store may receive three different calls from La Coruña in one week from a market specialist in each channel; a factory making shirts may deal simultaneously with two Zara managers, one for men's shirts and another for children's shirts. Though it's more expensive to operate three channels, the information flow for each channel is fast, direct, and unencumbered by problems in other channels—making the overall supply chain more responsive.

In each hall, floor to ceiling windows overlooking the Spanish countryside reinforce a sense of cheery informality and openness. Unlike companies that sequester their design staffs, Zara's cadre of 200 designers sits right in the midst of the production process. Split among the three lines, these mostly twentysomething designers—hired because of their enthusiasm and talent, no prima donnas allowed—work next to the market specialists and procurement and production planners. Large circular tables play host to impromptu meetings. Racks of the latest fashion magazines and catalogs fill the walls. A small prototype shop has been set up in the corner of each hall, which encourages everyone to comment on new garments as they evolve.

The physical and organizational proximity of the three groups increases both the speed and the quality of the design process. Designers can quickly and informally check initial sketches with colleagues. Market specialists, who are in constant touch with store managers (and many of whom have been store managers themselves), provide quick feedback about the look of the new designs (style, color, fabric, and so on) and suggest possible market price points. Procurement and production planners make preliminary, but crucial, estimates of manufacturing costs and available capacity. The cross-functional teams can examine prototypes in the hall, choose a design, and commit resources for its production and introduction in a few hours, if necessary.

Zara is careful about the way it deploys the latest information technology tools to facilitate these informal exchanges. Customized handheld computers support the connection between the retail stores and La Coruña. These PDAs augment regular (often weekly) phone conversations between the store managers and the market specialists assigned to them. Through the PDAs and telephone conversations, stores transmit all kinds of information to La Coruña—such hard data as orders and sales trends and such soft data as customer reactions and the "buzz" around a new style. While any company can use PDAs to communicate, Zara's flat organization ensures that important conversations don't fall through the bureaucratic cracks.

Once the team selects a prototype for production, the designers refine colors and textures on a computer-aided design system. If the item is to be made in one of Zara's factories, they transmit the specs directly to the relevant cutting machines and other systems in that factory. Bar codes track the cut pieces as they are converted into garments through the various steps involved in production (including sewing operations usually done by subcontractors), distribution, and delivery to the stores, where the communication cycle began.

The constant flow of updated data mitigates the so-called bullwhip effect—the tendency of supply chains (and all open-loop information systems) to amplify small disturbances. A small change in retail orders, for example, can result in wide fluctuations in factory orders after it's transmitted through wholesalers and distributors. In an industry that traditionally allows retailers to change a maximum of 20% of their orders once the season has started, Zara lets them adjust 40% to 50%. In this way, Zara avoids costly overproduction and the subsequent sales and discounting prevalent in the industry.

The relentless introduction of new products in small quantities, ironically, reduces the usual costs associated with running out of any particular item. Indeed, Zara makes a virtue of stock-outs. Empty racks don't drive customers to other stores because shoppers always have new things to choose from. Being out of stock in one item helps sell another, since people are often happy to snatch what they can. In fact, Zara has an informal policy of moving unsold items after two or three weeks. This can be an expensive practice for a typical store, but since Zara stores receive small shipments and carry little inventory, the risks are small; unsold items account for less than 10% of stock, compared with the industry average of 17% to 20%. Furthermore, new merchandise displayed in limited quantities and the short window of opportunity for purchasing items motivate people to visit Zara's shops more frequently than they might other stores. Consumers in central London, for example, visit the average store four times annually, but Zara's customers visit its shops an average of 17 times a year. The high traffic in the stores circumvents the need for advertising: Zara devotes just 0.3% of its sales on ads, far less than the 3% to 4% its rivals spend.

Stick to a Rhythm

Zara relinquishes control over very little in its supply chain—much less than its competitors. It designs and distributes all its products, outsources a smaller portion of its manufacturing than its peers, and owns nearly all its retail shops. Even Benetton, long recognized as a pioneer in tight supply chain management, does not extend its reach as far as Zara does. Most of Benetton's stores are franchises, and that gives it less sway over retail inventories and limits its direct access to the critical last step in the supply chain—the customers.

This level of control allows Zara to set the pace at which products and information flow. The entire chain moves to a fast but predictable rhythm that resembles Toyota's "*Takt* time" for assembly or the "inventory velocity" of Dell's procurement, production, and distribution system. By carefully timing the whole chain, Zara avoids the usual problem of rushing through one step and waiting to take the next.

The precise rhythm begins in the retail shops. Store managers in Spain and southern Europe place orders twice weekly, by 3:00 PM Wednesday and 6:00 PM Saturday, and the rest of the world places them by

3:00 PM Tuesday and 6:00 PM Friday. These deadlines are strictly enforced: If a store in Barcelona misses the Wednesday deadline, it has to wait until Saturday.

Order fulfillment follows the same strict rhythm. A central warehouse in La Coruña prepares the shipments for every store, usually overnight. Once loaded onto a truck, the boxes and racks are either rushed to a nearby airport or routed directly to the European stores. All trucks and connecting airfreights run on established schedules—like a bus service—to match the retailers' twice-weekly orders. Shipments reach most European stores in 24 hours, U.S. stores in 48 hours, and Japanese shops in 72 hours, so store managers know exactly when the shipments will come in.

When the trucks arrive at the stores, the rapid rhythm continues. Because all the items have already been prepriced and tagged, and most are shipped hung up on racks, store managers can put them on display the moment they're delivered, without having to iron them. The need for control at this stage is minimized because the shipments are 98.9% accurate with less than 0.5% shrinkage. Finally, because regular customers know exactly when the new deliveries come, they visit the stores more frequently on those days.

This relentless and transparent rhythm aligns all the players in Zara's supply chain. It guides daily decisions by managers, whose job is to ensure that nothing hinders the responsiveness of the total system. It reinforces the production of garments in small batches, though larger batches would reduce costs. It validates the company policy of delivering two shipments every week, though less frequent shipment would reduce distribution costs. It justifies transporting products by air and truck, though ships and trains would lower transportation fees. And it provides a rationale for shipping some garments on hangers, though folding them into boxes would reduce the air and truck freight charges.

These counterintuitive practices pay off. Zara has shown that by maintaining a strict rhythm, it can carry less inventory (about 10% of sales, compared to 14% to 15% at Benetton, H&M, and Gap); maintain a higher profit margin on sales; and grow its revenues.

Leverage Your Assets

In a volatile market where product life cycles are short, it's better to own fewer assets—thus goes the conventional wisdom shared by many senior managers, stock analysts, and management gurus. Zara subverts this logic. It produces roughly half of its products in its own factories. It buys 40% of its fabric from another Inditex firm, Comditel (accounting for almost 90% of Comditel's total sales), and it purchases its dyestuff from yet another Inditex company. So much vertical integration is clearly out of fashion in the industry; rivals like Gap and H&M, for example, own no production facilities. But Zara's managers reason that investment in capital assets can actually increase the organization's overall flexibility. Owning production assets gives Zara a level of control over schedules and capacities that, its senior managers argue, would be impossible to achieve if the company were entirely dependent on outside suppliers, especially ones located on the other side of the world.

The simpler products, like sweaters in classic colors, are outsourced to suppliers in Europe, North Africa, and Asia. But Zara reserves the manufacture of the more-complicated products, like women's suits in new seasonal colors, for its own factories (18 of which are in La Coruña, two in Barcelona, and one in Lithuania, with a few joint ventures in other countries). When Zara produces a garment in-house, it uses local subcontractors for simple and labor-intensive steps of the production process, like sewing. These are small workshops, each with only a few dozen employees, and Zara is their primary customer.

Zara can ramp up or down production of specific garments quickly and conveniently because it normally operates many of its factories for only a single shift. These highly automated factories can operate extra hours if need be to meet seasonal or unforeseen demands. Specialized by garment type, Zara's factories use sophisticated just-in-time systems, developed in cooperation with Toyota, that allow the company to customize its processes and exploit innovations. For example, like Benetton, Zara uses "postponement" to gain more speed and flexibility, purchasing more than 50% of its fabrics undyed so that it can react faster to midseason color changes.

All finished products pass through the five-story, 500,000-square-meter distribution center in La Coruña, which ships approximately 2.5 million items per week. There, the allocation of such resources as floor space, layout, and equipment follows the same logic that Zara applies to its factories. Storing and shipping many of its pieces on racks, for instance, requires extra warehouse space and elaborate material-handling equipment. Operating hours follow the weekly rhythm of the orders: In a normal week, this facility functions around the clock for four days but runs for only one or two shifts on the remaining three days. Ordinarily, 800 people fill the orders, each within eight hours. But during peak seasons, the company adds as many as 400 temporary staffers to maintain lead times.

Even though there's ample capacity in this distribution center during most of the year, Zara opened a new €100 million, 120,000-square-meter logistics center in Zaragoza, northeast of Madrid, in October 2003. Why is Zara so generous with capacity? Zara's senior managers follow a fundamental rule of queuing models, which holds that waiting time shoots up exponentially when capacity is tight and demand is variable (see the exhibit "For fast response, have extra capacity on hand"). By tolerating lower capacity utilization in its factories and distribution centers, Zara can react to peak or unexpected demands faster than its rivals.

Surprisingly, these practices don't burn up investment dollars. Thanks to the responsiveness of its factories and distribution centers, Zara has dramatically reduced its need for working capital. Because the company can sell its products just a few days after they're made, it can operate with negative working capital. The cash thus freed up helps offset the investment in extra capacity.

For fast response, have extra capacity on hand

Zara's senior managers seem to comprehend intuitively the nonlinear relationship between capacity utilization, demand variability, and responsiveness. This relationship is well demonstrated by "queuing theory"—which explains that as capacity utilization begins to increase from low levels, waiting times increase gradually. But at some point, as the system uses more of the available capacity, waiting times accelerate rapidly. As demand becomes ever more variable, this acceleration starts at lower and lower levels of capacity utilization.

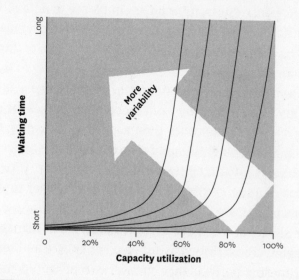

Reinforcing Principles

None of the three principles outlined above—closing the communication loop, sticking to a rhythm, and leveraging your assets—is particularly new or radical. Each one alone could improve the responsiveness of any company's supply chain. But together, they create a powerful force because they reinforce one another. When a company is organized for direct, quick, and rich communications among those who manage its supply chain, it's easier to set a steady rhythm. Conversely, a strict schedule for moving information and goods through the supply chain makes it easier for operators at different steps to communicate with one another. And when the company focuses its own capital assets on responsiveness, it becomes simpler to maintain this rhythm. These principles, devotedly applied over many years, help to put together the jigsaw puzzle of Zara's practices.

Perhaps the deepest secret of Zara's success is its ability to sustain an environment that optimizes the entire supply chain rather than each step. Grasping the full implication of this approach is a big challenge. Few managers can imagine sending a half-empty truck across Europe, paying for airfreight twice a week to ship coats on hangers to Japan, or running factories for only one shift. But this is exactly why Zara's senior managers deserve credit. They have stayed the course and resisted setting performance measures that would make their operating managers focus on local efficiency at the expense of global responsiveness. They have hardwired into the organization the lesson Ortega learned almost 30 years ago: Touch the factories and customers with two hands. Do everything possible to let one hand help the other. And whatever you do, don't take your eyes off the product until it's sold.

KASRA FERDOWS is the Heisley Family Professor of Global Manufacturing at Georgetown University in Washington, DC. **MICHAEL A. LEWIS** is a professor of operations and supply management at the University of Bath School of Management in the UK. **JOSE A.D. MACHUCA** is a professor of operations management at the University of Seville in Spain.

Originally published in November 2004. Reprint R0411G

Supply Chain Challenges: Building Relationships

A Conversation with Scott Beth, David N. Burt, William Copacino, Chris Gopal, Hau L. Lee, Robert Porter Lynch, and Sandra Morris

SUPPLY CHAIN MANAGEMENT IS ALL about software and systems, right? Get the best technology in place, then sit back and watch as your processes run smoothly and the savings roll in.

If that's true, then why did Jeff Bezos raid Wal-Mart's bench, paying top dollar to bring best-in-class logistics expertise to Amazon? Supply chains, it seems, are really about talent, not technology, especially as the marketplace grows ever more complex. But how to get people to work together?

It's not easy. When *Harvard Business Review* recently convened a panel of leading thinkers in the field of supply chain management, people and relationships were the dominant topics of the day. Creating effective alliances between companies, for instance, is complicated. Purchasing managers are rewarded for wringing the best possible price out of suppliers—a practice that's not conducive to nurturing long-standing partnerships. Internal relationships can be even more difficult to manage, according to one of our panelists. We've long known that functional silos hinder communication and efficiency, but many companies still struggle to tear down the walls.

Our panel, led by HBR senior editor Julia Kirby, explored these and such other obstacles and opportunities in supply chain management as developing talent, the role of the chief executive, and the latest technologies. The few companies that have cracked these nuts are gaining ground: The gap between the supply chain leaders and the average performers is large and growing. The following is an edited transcript of the panel's conversation.

Julia Kirby: *I suspect that priorities in supply chain management have changed quite a bit in the last couple of years, for a variety of reasons. There's the economic downturn and the plunge into overcapacity. There's also terrorism and war. So I'd like to start by asking, What are the priorities today? Has your focus changed?*

Chris Gopal: One area that's quite different from what it was a few years ago is, of course, security. The government has imposed, and is in the process of imposing, new regulations and requirements, particularly on companies doing business overseas, and a lot of them

Idea in Brief

Supply chain management is all about software and systems, right? Put in the best technology, sit back, and watch as your processes run smoothly and the savings roll in? Apparently not. When HBR convened a panel of leading thinkers in the field of supply chain management, technology was not top of mind. People and relationships were the dominant issues of the day. The opportunities and problems created by globalization, for example, are requiring companies to establish relationships with new types of suppliers. The ever-present pressure for speed and cost containment is making it even more important to break down stubbornly high internal barriers and establish more effective cross-functional relationships. The costs of failure have never been higher.

The leading supply chain performers are applying new technology, new innovations, and process thinking to far greater advantage than the laggards, reaping tremendous gains in all the variables that affect shareholder value: cost, customer service, asset productivity, and revenue generation. And the gap between the leaders and the losers is growing in almost every industry. This roundtable gathered many of the leading thinkers and doers in the field of supply chain management, including practitioners Scott Beth of Intuit, Sandra Morris of Intel, and Chris Gopal of Unisys. David Burt of the University of San Diego and Stanford's Hau Lee bring the latest research from academia. Accenture's William Copacino and the Warren Co.'s Robert Porter Lynch offer the consultant's perspectives.

are not prepared for it. We've all heard about the stories of a ship being held up at a major port—at Long Beach, California, say—because it's got cargo that has set off alarm bells.

Another current priority is getting the tools we need to create an adaptive and responsive supply chain strategy—which is important because most supply chain strategies start down the road to being obsolete almost as soon as they're published. Creating an adaptive strategy starts with modeling the supply chain and doing scenario planning. That allows you to more effectively manage risk and cope with changes and uncertainty in the market, which in turn increases cash flow and customer retention. And then, once you execute your strategy, you need to be able to redo it based on patterns and trends derived from real-time information. Companies need tools for this kind of continual innovation—and there are none today.

Sandra Morris: A big shift for Intel has been globalization. Our customer base is changing dramatically, not just in terms of where they live but also who they are and how they operate. There's huge potential in China, for example, and growing markets in Russia and India. That drives a different type of supply chain requirement. For example, the companies that are building and shipping PCs in emerging markets are small resellers, small distributors, not the typical multinational corporation we've worked with for decades. Their needs are different.

William Copacino: If you think back three to five years, the major issue for many companies was not to run out of parts. Today we have significant global overcapacity in most industries. So a key issue is managing the supply base—including sourcing, supplier integration, and in-bound parts management.

I also see a shift in focus from planning to execution. But I personally believe that there are huge opportunities on the planning side—in matching supply and demand. People are missing out because their attention, frankly, is so focused at the transactional level. We are seeing a shift back to basics—to MES [manufacturing execution systems] and WMS [warehouse management systems].

And we are beginning to see a growing interest in radio frequency identification—RFID—for several reasons. The cost of both chips and reader-writers is coming down rapidly, so the cost of solutions is becoming more competitive; the capabilities are expanding; and the need is growing in areas like theft protection and security.

Scott Beth: A big issue for us is misalignment of materials technologies and product life cycles. Say you're building instrumentation products that will last ten to 15 years using semiconductor components and other materials that may be available in the market for only 18 to 36 months before they're discontinued. This situation presents me with three alternatives: I have to buy and store a 13-year supply of components—that's a lot of extra inventory. Or I'm forced to mortgage the future by pulling engineers off new product development to reengineer products that still have a life in the marketplace. Or I have to find brokers or others who are willing to take the risk of holding onto unique and rapidly aging parts.

Kirby: *I'm struck that I'm not hearing you say, "Three years ago, the whole point of supply chain management was to increase speed, and now we're totally focused on cost reduction." Is that not happening?*

Robert Porter Lynch: To some extent, it is. The most disturbing trend that I've seen, with the meltdown of

The Panelists (Alphabetical order)

Scott Beth is the vice president of procurement at Intuit. At the time of the roundtable, Beth was a senior director of global sourcing for Agilent Technologies' electronic products and solutions group.

David N. Burt is a professor of supply chain management and the director of the University of San Diego's Institute of Supply Chain Management.

William Copacino is the group chief executive of Accenture's Business Consulting capability group. He is the author of several books on supply chain management, including *Supply Chain Management: The Basics and Beyond* (St. Lucie Press, 1997).

Chris Gopal is the vice president of global supply chain management at Unisys. Previously he was the director of global supply chain consulting at Ernst & Young and a vice president at Dell Computer.

Hau L. Lee is the Thoma Professor of Operations, Information, and Technology at Stanford University, codirector of the Stanford Global Supply Chain Management Forum, and director of the Managing Your Supply Chain for Global Competitiveness Executive Program.

Robert Porter Lynch is the CEO of the Warren Company. He is the author of *Business Alliances Guide: The Hidden Competitive Weapon* (Wiley, 1993).

Sandra Morris is a vice president and the chief information officer of Intel, where she has been since 1985. Previously, she was at the David Sarnoff Research Center of RCA.

---

the stock market, has been cost cutting as a knee-jerk reaction. A chief financial officer will call the supply officer and say, "Cut costs 15%; we've got to get our stock price up." That knee-jerk reaction is having wholesale effects throughout the supply chain in very negative ways. You start to see cost cutting become a substitute for much more important competitive-advantage issues. A principle in business is that you cut costs to survive, but you innovate to prosper.

Beth: We're under incredible pressure to reduce material costs. But just as much on my mind is dealing with suppliers who aren't going to make it through this business downturn—many basic-component manufacturers are going out of business. When you're relying on a partner for unique technology, what do you do when they say they're locking their doors next week? How do you (a) find another source and (b) predict the health of suppliers so you can anticipate a shortfall before it happens?

Hau L. Lee: Cost is important, and so is speed. But I and my colleagues have been studying companies that have been hugely successful in the long run. And we've discovered that those companies are great not because they were focused on cost or flexibility or speed but because they have the ability to manage transitions—changing market conditions, evolving technology, different requirements as a product moves through its life cycle. The companies that can adapt are, I think, the ones that will be here for the long term.

These days, companies also need to be able to handle one more type of transition, which is crisis management. Successful companies have been able to grab market share and sales out of crises, which often requires them to work effectively across functional boundaries. I cite you the example of Zara, a Spanish apparel company. After September 11, which was, of course, a time of mourning, this company was able to get its designers, supply chain partners, and manufacturers together and in two weeks launch a new line of apparel featuring the color black. They got a tremendous sales lift as a result.

Companies like that have what I call the triple-A supply chain. They have agility, adaptability, and alignment. You need to align the interests of the functional groups and multiple partners so that you will be able to move forward in unison.

Kirby: *But we've known for 15 years that functional silos get in the way. Are the barriers starting to come down at all?*

Lee: I still find many big corporations where each of the different functions do not know what the others are doing. A company might have promotion plans or a special trade deal in place, and the supply chain people are unaware of it. Or the supply chain manager plans how much inventory to put in place or how much capacity to invest in and doesn't share that with the sales and marketing people. And so you may find yourself in a situation where the sales and marketing people are giving special deals on a particular product when, in fact, you're running up to the capacity limit.

There are a lot of great examples of this disconnect. The most celebrated is Volvo, which made a lot of green cars in 1995 and wasn't able to sell them. So the sales and marketing people started to secretly offer heavy discounts, rebates, and special deals on green cars to their dealerships. The supply chain people didn't know that, and when they saw the green cars selling, they doubled their production plan for them for the next year. Volvo had a lot of green cars at the end of that year.

Morris: We've created a capability—five people, very senior program managers, who can look horizontally across functions. They bring together executives or senior managers and facilitate discussions about the tensions between product division goals, supply network goals, and customer goals. We have lots of people who are deep in their silos. They're also really smart. So getting them together on a fairly regular basis to deal with strategic topics in a facilitated session has been a breakthrough for us. It's probably been one of the best investments we've made.

Lynch: Here's a data point. I'm the chairman emeritus of the Association of Alliance Professionals, and we did a survey last year of the critical issues concerning strategic alliance professionals throughout the world. We have 800 members. The number one concern these professionals had wasn't creating strategic alliances with other companies but creating alliances internally between the silos of their own company. For some reason, alliance professionals typically find it easier to create alliances with their major competitors than with other divisions in their own companies. We don't deal with our own internal integration. How do we integrate externally if we can't do it internally?

Gopal: Way back in 1980, some studies were done as to why MRP [manufacturing resource planning] systems failed in implementation. One of the key reasons was this concept of silos, individual departments with their own metrics. To illustrate this, they came up with something called the Beer Game, in which you simulate a sudden change in demand and need to get your supply chain back into equilibrium. So now I'm sitting here in 2003 listening to exactly the same point and exactly the same comment about what makes these relationships successful. Has anything changed? Are we still dealing with the same problems in different forms?

Copacino: Some companies are. But I think there's been a tremendous bifurcation of performance. In almost every industry, supply chain has become a much more important strategic and competitive variable. It affects all of the shareholder value levers—cost, customer service, asset productivity, and revenue generation. Yet we are seeing a growing gap in performance between the leading and the average companies. The best are getting better faster than the average companies across almost every industry. For instance from 1995 to 2001, Wal-Mart improved its inventory turns from 5.23 to 8.34. Its nearest competitor over that same time moved from 4.01 to just above five inventory turns, not even to the point where Wal-Mart started. And Dell operates with 64 to 100 inventory turns, more than two or three times most of its competitors. So, clearly, the performance gap is widening, and we see this happening in almost every industry segment.

The leading supply chain performers are applying new technology, new innovations, and new process thinking to great advantage. The average-performing companies and the laggards have a limited window of opportunity in which to catch up.

Kirby: *Robert mentioned that companies are having an easier time with external alliances than with internal ones. How are those external relationships evolving?*

Lynch: The best companies I see are beginning to triage the supply chain. In other words, they'll separate vendors that provide commodities from preferred suppliers that they have good relationships with from strategic suppliers that they create alliances with. They manage the supply base through those three different elements in very different ways, using different metrics, different processes, different people, and different mentalities.

Beth: Absolutely. I think that we have to determine, in Intel's case, where contract manufacturers fall along that spectrum. Speaking frankly, I think there's a love-hate relationship between OEMs and contract manufacturers. People don't trust the pricing they get, or there's a sort of bait-and-switch approach, where your prices start out low and then begin to creep up.

Kirby: *David, I see you nodding at this reference to trust. I know that issue is dear to your heart. What can you add?*

David N. Burt: Trust is the basis of agility, of flexibility. Yet it's an incredible challenge to establish trust and maybe even harder to maintain it. Underlying the challenge is the question of how to institutionalize trust between buyer and supplier. I've got colleagues who maintain that trust can only be established between individuals. But a few souls like Robert and myself say we've got to be able to institutionalize trust. We've got to make it work so that when the founders of the alliance depart, the alliance continues. We've been looking at this at USD for over ten years, and we don't have the answer yet.

But it's important. As the world gets more complicated, when I sell a product, I may be selling a solution that requires input from four or five companies. How do they get along with each other? If suppliers don't trust each other, the customer will be whipsawed. Also, trust enables you to make fast decisions, which lets you be more innovative and get rid of unproductive work. Trust is a competitive advantage.

Beth: You also lose out on efficiencies when trust isn't there. A lack of trust causes companies to duplicate activities between its own operations and its outsourced partners. Too often, we outsource an activity and then keep a lot of the management systems for that activity in place to verify that certain things are being done.

Lee: The way to build trust and establish a harmonious relationship is the third A of my triple-A: alignment—align the interests of the multiple parties so that they have some common values and goals.

A good example of alignment comes from Saturn. Saturn recognized that to provide good service in terms of the end customer's experience, it wouldn't be enough to be good at replenishing and supporting dealerships, which Saturn calls "retailers." The retailers also needed to have the right inventory. But Saturn understood that the retailers weren't necessarily good at inventory planning and forecasting. So the company asked retailers to let it take over the job of inventory management, and in return it offered to share their risk. If you're out of stock, Saturn will get the part to you from another retailer, overnight. Saturn even measures its own employees on how well the retailers serve their customers, the end users.

The result is that Saturn is always ranked among the top three in J.D. Power's Customer Satisfaction Index, even though it's competing with luxury cars. And Saturn retailers have a superior inventory performance— its average dealer inventory turn is about 7.5 a year versus the industry average of 2.5. Everybody wins when you have the right alignment.

Gopal: I'd like to add a slightly different perspective. Trust is essential, of course. But before trust comes smart contracting. Trust is predicated on doing things jointly and in an aligned fashion over a period of time with no major surprises. However, to start with, the supply chain folks, who know the environment and the potential risks, need to get together with the people who develop the contracts so that managing risk— planning for alternative scenarios—can be embedded in the strategy and the contract. The next step is metrics. Trust can only be engendered by considering the risks and having joint metrics, with penalties and incentives. And over time, trust develops. I know that Scott does a lot of work in managing risk, working with different types of contracts with suppliers to generate some of that trust. Scott, do you have anything to tell us about this?

Beth: Our expectations for suppliers are changing. In the past, the contract manager would put a contract in front of me and point to a 3% price reduction over last year. The vector is right, and it's my only choice, so I'd sign off on it. But now what I expect is a series of choices that trade off price, inventory, and responsiveness. Those are the kinds of trade-offs that I need to be able to think about.

But on the issue of trust and penalties: We started off with a penalty approach, a clause that says if you don't provide us with a certain level of responsiveness, we'll charge you. And that began to erode trust. So instead we created an escrow account. If either party violates the agreement, money goes into the account, which is then used to reinvest in the relationship—new information systems, joint team education, and travel to get our people together more often. The level of trust went way up when we took this change in perspective.

Burt: These types of contracts and processes are critical. A company in our benchmark study—a large consumer products company—buys, for example, enzymes for its soap from a small company in Denmark. There are numerous intellectual property issues related to developing new chemical enzyme technologies, so naturally there are concerns about sharing ideas. The two companies worked out master agreements ahead of time so that they could develop and share new technologies without always having to go back to the lawyers and sign new legal agreements. They both placed a great deal of emphasis on ethics and had a clear under-standing about the procedures, about what was ex-pected from whom. The relationship was so good, and Natalie, the supply chain manager from the American company, fought so hard within her company on behalf of the supplier, that the Danish company named its latest enzyme Natalese for her.

So the relationship counts, but so does the process. They had a clear process governing how to work to-gether, which allowed them to be constantly innovating and kept the relationship healthy.

Morris: I agree that good contracts are absolutely es-sential, but we've also seen that you can develop trust over time by increasing access to information and to ex-perts within the company. That's particularly been the case with our e-business efforts, such as automatic re-plenishment of the factories. It starts with a pilot, with one trusted supplier, and it grows over time to become the standard way we do business.

We've watched the same kind of relationship grow among suppliers as we've created information reposito-ries for fabrication equipment. When we develop a new technology, we work for years and years with both our customers and our suppliers before that technology is available, so products exist that use the technology when it's ready to ship. That sometimes involves a number of suppliers sharing information with each other as well as with Intel. The process, which began with three or four people who were willing to take that risk with us—to be fellow travelers—has now become a common way that we exchange information and develop new products.

Lynch: Picking up on the idea of sharing with your partners in the value chain, there's an avenue of innovation that's just being completely missed, which is innovations that come from your suppliers. Dr. Burt did a study on this; I believe it was last year. And I think the average company said that 35% of its innovation came from the supply chain. Now, ask yourself, is that enough? Companies like Toyota are getting 60% of all their innovation out of the supply chain.

Here's a story. A client told me, "My largest customer is Johnson & Johnson. Every year, they come to me and they want a 5% to 15% price cut. I have piles of innovation to bring them. Every time I ask the supply chain manager, 'What about my innovations? Where do I take them?' He says, 'I'm not interested in that.' Why not? Because he's not rewarded for innovation. He's rewarded for cost cutting."

Another example: If you look at General Motors during the 1990s, warranty costs were higher than profits. Why were warranty costs so high? A lot of it is because GM wasn't looking to the supply chain for innovation. Chrysler, meanwhile, took massive amounts of market share because it was taking innovation through the supply chain. So, the question is, Do we prize it? Do we even measure it? Do we recognize the impact of supplier innovation on our competitive advantage? On customer satisfaction?

Gopal: I'd like to go a level below all of that and say the companies I've seen that innovate best in the supply chain seem to be those that actually have the excellent people focused on the supply chain. I think it's a people issue, an issue of senior management focus and will. Michael Dell and his senior executives used to attend demand/supply-matching meetings. Dell executives are measured on joint metrics—they are (or at least they used to be) all measured on the same things—and that drives their focus on the supply chain as a competitive weapon.

Somebody once asked me about best practices. Well, knowledge is free. Everything that Dell, Wal-Mart, and 7-Eleven do is available somewhere on the Internet. Yet how many people can actually execute on it? The key is putting the system together right and making sure it works—managing risks and planning for contingencies through scenario planning, then executing and changing the strategy based on real-time trends.

Somebody also asked me about worst practices. I think the absolute worst practice is equating technology with the supply chain—the idea that "I buy a technology, so I've got a great supply chain." Nonsense. Innovation comes down to the people, the tools, and what value senior management places on it. I'd like to ask Hau, How many students at Stanford go into management of the supply chain?

Kirby: *I think a lot of people woke up to the talent component of supply chain management when Amazon quite visibly and famously raided Wal-Mart's supply chain management talent. That was a surprise to a lot of people who thought supply chain was mainly about technology and how much money you spent on distribution center design and the like. But is it really about talent, Hau?*

Lee: I agree that people—and in particular the leadership—are a very important part of supply chain management. Toshifumi Suzuki, the chairman of Seven-Eleven Japan, spends a whole morning each week reviewing the previous week's supply chain performance. It shows his passion, and it shows his commitment and interest.

In terms of our students at Stanford, electives on supply chain used to be unpopular, but now we have to offer more sections. I know my colleagues at other schools are seeing the same thing. And it's because we have companies like Dell, Seven-Eleven Japan, and Zara that are hiring talented people and giving them opportunities for a great career path, showing them that supply chain is not about just managing within these four walls. And the difference is not in cost containment but in innovation and value creation.

Kirby: *Scott, are you seeing that? Is your talent pool rising?*

Beth: Yes. When I meet with a group of procurement professionals, I ask them about their backgrounds. In the past, I got primarily teachers, real estate agents, accountants, administrators, political scientists, sometimes a lawyer or two. Now I'm finding the population shifting toward supply chain professionals, people who are coming with that training.

Kirby: *So talent is key. But what about technology? Is it not as fundamental as some people believe?*

Burt: There are two schools of thought. One is that by getting the right software we can get rid of people. It's that simple. The other is that IT and other technologies are enablers, and they can be tremendous assets when you have the right people in place. But if your CEO or CFO thinks that you're going to get rid of people because you bought whatever software, I'm not sure it's a place you want to work.

Morris: Some amazing information technology has arrived on the scene, RosettaNet being one in the PC supply chain. It's a story of incredible cooperation among competitors—400 companies got together to define business processes at a pretty tactical level. How do we treat an order? How do we treat a return? How do we treat an advance-shipping notice? What fields do we need so that we can have machine-to-machine communication, allowing a distributor to connect to 35 suppliers and not have to create point-to-point business processes and reconcile data on the back end on a daily basis?

Last year, we did about 10% of our transactions with customers using the RosettaNet standard. I don't think it will completely replace EDI, but we think over time it will become a standard way for us to connect, for certain types of transactions. It's more efficient, not because we think we can lower head count but because we can get people out of the day-to-day business of reconciling and touching purchase orders that should never be touched and get them to focus on higher-order service and strategies for the company.

Lee: Technology—hardware as well as software—is without question crucial in supply chain management. But technology can break the company as well as enable the company to be hugely successful. The distinction is in how people use their technology. Technology is an enabler. You can turn it into power and then receive C-level attention. It depends on the people.

Copacino: One of the critical findings out of our research was exactly that: The masters—the leading companies—are extraordinarily good at selectively choosing what technologies to implement. Others—the average-performing companies and the laggards—are broader and less selective in deciding what technology solutions to implement. And the masters are very disciplined in their implementation, focusing on process design and effective program management and change management.

Lynch: I would add that companies are much more cautious now about technology because there were so many implementation bungles that drove companies up the wall. They are now much more careful to make sure that an implementation is going to go according to plan and it's going to meet the company's needs. Whereas three or four years ago, so many companies were implementing technology willy-nilly because they thought it was a cure-all.

Kirby: *What about RFID? Is it real? Is it overhyped? What's the ROI horizon?*

Copacino: We have seen a significant pickup in interest and successful pilots over the last six months. As prices come down, with chip prices that are now approaching 20 cents and will over time go to five cents, RFID becomes very valuable from a productivity point of view. Price points are coming down on reading equipment, too.

We are actively working on probably nine or ten applications, particularly in areas where there's concern about theft. But, more fundamentally, we're also seeing broader efficiency and operational improvements over traditional processes, methods, and technologies.

Gopal: The application is everywhere. Retail is one. Ford uses a real-time logistics system for visibility through triangulation. Container people use it for tracking. And I think, with Operation Safe Commerce, now it's going to be even more in demand. Adoption will go by industry. Five cents is a good-enough price point for some heavy industrial manufacturing. One cent will be good enough for very low-margin consumables, maybe. It's a question of economics and end-to-end visibility.

Lee: I think RFID will evolve much as e-commerce has evolved. When e-commerce first came out, it just automated existing processes and work flows. You could send a purchase order by the Internet or pay an invoice or communicate through e-mail. You were substituting an existing technology for a new one, but you were doing the same thing.

That's not the biggest impact of e-commerce. As Sandra described, the biggest value comes when you can do things like collaborate with your suppliers, as Microsoft did when it used the Internet to collaborate on the design for the Xbox. And you can also use e-commerce to change a process. For example, e-commerce can allow manufacturers to ship products directly to consumers, bypassing multiple layers of distribution channels. It's the process changes that create the greater value.

RFID will follow the same kind of evolution. Now it's mostly tracking. Instead of physically counting how many items you have on the shelf, the technology can read it, and you know instantly. You want to find out when an item left the store? You know instantly. This is automating an existing process that you're currently doing manually. That's the first level but not the biggest impact. I think the biggest value will come from new applications that use the technology's intelligence. RFID can create a borderless supply chain when cargoes are equipped with tags showing the contents, so that customs clearance can be done almost automatically. RFID can also provide supply chain security when RFID tags are used to electronically seal containers and monitor movements of the containers, so that any tampering can be tracked.

Kirby: *I have one more question, which touches on a number of things we've talked about today—sharing information with customers and suppliers, developing alliances, innovating with suppliers. My question is, When do we stop talking about the supply chain and start talking about the value chain?*

Lynch: The problem with value chain is that most people haven't really started to think about it. It's not taught in the university; we don't have a value chain professor. It's like strategic alliances: It sort of grew organically. But in many industries, the leaders actually have shifted from supply chain to value chain, even if they haven't branded it that. Look at what Wal-Mart did to Kmart. That's a value chain story, not just supply chain. Some other companies are very good at managing the value chain as well. Southwest Airlines has it figured all the way out from the customer right back through the whole chain. Dell Computer is managing the chain from the customer all the way back through the supply networks. Another is Harley-Davidson. And Saturn, as Hau showed us.

I'm going to predict that within five years, we will have the battle of the value chains. And then it will shift to value networks after that.

Burt: Robert, I know it's always dangerous to disagree with you, but I'll put myself in jeopardy and point out that our recently approved master of science in supply chain management has a capstone course called Value Chain Management.

Gopal: I look at value chains and supply chains almost synonymously, and I'm trying to figure out the difference. The word "value" is one that I fundamentally distrust, having been burned by it in so many different environments. And I'm trying to figure out what you mean when you talk about value chain versus supply chain. Are they really different? I don't buy "new-name proliferation."

Copacino: You get into semantics on this. I was asked by the Council of Logistics Management to develop a definition of supply chain and logistics. We had six prominent people on the committee I formed, and we could not agree on a single definition.

But I take the same perspective that Chris does. I think that supply chain done right is a value chain. It's an integrated supply and demand chain or an integrated value chain. When you think about it that way, you use it to drive revenues and innovation and create value—not just to reduce cost. And that's where you start to get strategic advantage.

Originally published in July 2003. Reprint R0307E

Leading a Supply Chain Turnaround

by Reuben E. Slone

THINGS WOULD BE VERY DIFFERENT TODAY—for me, my colleagues, and my company—if the votes of Whirlpool's North American leadership team had swung in a different direction on May 3, 2001. It was a move I hadn't expected; Mike Todman, our executive vice president at the time, decided to go around the table and ask each member of his staff for a thumbs-up or thumbs-down on the investment that Paul Dittmann and I had just formally proposed. Did I look worried? I can't imagine I didn't, even though we'd spent hours in individual meetings with each of them, getting their ideas and buy-in. We thought we had everyone's support. But the facts remained: Our proposal had a bigger price tag than any supply chain investment in the company's history. We were asking for tens of millions during a period of general belt-tightening. Some of it was slated for new hires, even as cutbacks were taking place elsewhere in the company. And Paul and I, the people doing the asking, were coming from the supply chain organization.

Let me be clear: The supply chain organization was the part of the business that Whirlpool's salespeople were in the habit of calling the "sales disablers" in 2000. We were perpetually behind the eight ball, tying up too much capital in finished goods inventory—yet failing to provide the product availability our customers needed. Our availability hovered around 87%. Our colleagues grimly joked that in surveys on the delivery performance of the four biggest appliance manufacturers in the U.S., we came in fifth.

And here, with all the credibility that track record conferred on us, we were proposing an ambitious new suite of IT solutions—something, too, for which the company had little appetite. It had been just 20 months since Whirlpool North America had flipped the switch on a massive new ERP system, with less than desired effect. Normally, Whirlpool ships close to 70,000 appliances a day to North American customers. The day after we went live with SAP, we were able to ship about 2,000. A barrage of bad press followed. Even though the situation was soon righted (SAP remains a valued partner), the experience of being treated as a sort of poster child for ERP folly had left scars.

So imagine our relief when we heard the first voice say "yes." It was the executive who headed up sales to Sears. Paul and I looked anxiously to the next face, and the next. The heads of our KitchenAid, Whirlpool, and value brands followed suit—a watershed, given that the funding would have to come from their budgets. I could

Idea in Brief

Just five years ago, salespeople at Whirlpool were in the habit of referring to their supply chain organization as the "sales disablers." Now the company excels at getting products to the right place at the right time while managing to keep inventories low. How did that happen? In this first-person account, Reuben Slone, Whirlpool's vice-president of global supply chain, describes how he and his colleagues devised the right supply chain strategy, sold it internally, and implemented it. Slone insisted that the right focal point for the strategy was the satisfaction of consumers at the end of the supply chain. Most supply chain initiatives do the opposite: They start with the realities of a company's manufacturing base and proceed from there. Through a series of interviews with trade customers large and small, his team identified 27 different

capabilities that drove industry perceptions of Whirlpool's performance. Knowing it was infeasible to aim for world-class performance across all of them, Slone weighed the costs of excelling at each and found the combination of initiatives that would provide overall competitive advantage. A highly disciplined project management office and broad training in project management were key to keeping work on budget and on benefit. Slone set an intense pace—three "releases" of new capabilities every month—that the group maintains to this day. Lest this seem like a technology story, however, Slone insists it is just as much a "talent renaissance." People are proud today to be part of Whirlpool's supply chain organization, and its new generation of talent will give the company a competitive advantage for years to come.

see that J.C. Anderson, my boss and senior vice president of operations, was happy, too. He had tried to voice his support at the beginning of the meeting, but Mike Todman had asked him to wait. Now that it was his turn to vote, he did it with a flourish: "I am fully committed," he said, "to moving our supply chain from a liability to a recognized competitive advantage." Only after Todman had heard from everyone in the room—brands, sales, finance, human resources, and operations—did he cast his vote.

With that last yes, the tension broke, and everyone was smiling and nodding. Paul and I had a sense of triumph—but also trepidation. Because now, we knew, there could be no excuses. We were on the hook to deliver some serious value.

Devising the Strategy

My responsibility at Whirlpool today is for the performance of the global supply chain. But in 2001, I was focused only on North America, and I was utterly new to the supply chain organization. (I had come into the company a few years earlier to lead its e-business efforts.) By contrast, Paul Dittmann, the vice president of supply chain strategy, was a Whirlpool veteran with a tenure spanning a quarter century.

Our lots were cast together in October 2000 by Jeff Fettig. Jeff is now Whirlpool's chairman and CEO, but at the time he was president and COO—and he was good and tired of hearing about spotty service and high logistics costs. Sales had risen to record levels in 2000 as our launch of some innovative products coincided with an uptick in housing starts. With the rest of the company chugging on all cylinders, there was only one thing holding us back: our supply chain. Jeff called me into his office and gave me a two-word order: "Fix it."

If that constitutes a mandate, we had one. But it was up to us to figure out what fixing the supply chain would entail. At the top level, of course, it's a simple formulation: getting the right product to the right place at the right time—*all* the time. That gets complicated very quickly, however, when you consider the scale of the challenge. Whirlpool makes a diverse line of washers, dryers, refrigerators, dishwashers, and ovens, with manufacturing facilities in 13 countries. We sell those appliances in 100 countries, through retailers big and small and to the construction companies and developers that build new homes. In the United States alone, our logistics network consists of eight factory distribution centers, ten regional distribution centers, 60 local distribution centers, and nearly 20,000 retail and contract customers.

We needed to formulate a battle plan that would include new information technology, processes, roles, and talents. But before we could begin to imagine those, we needed to define our strategy. Looking to the future, what would it mean to be world-class in supply chain performance?

The decision we made at this very early point in the process was, I think, a pivotal one. We decided that we could answer that question only by focusing on customer requirements first. Our approach to developing our supply chain strategy would be to start with the last link—the consumer—and proceed backward.

It's an obvious thought, isn't it? Except that it wasn't. The overwhelming tendency in a manufacturing organization is to think about the supply chain as something that originates with the supply base and moves forward. It's understandable: This is the part of the chain over which the company has control. But the unfortunate effect is that supply chain initiatives typically run out of steam before they get to their end point—and real point. Whether or not they make customers' lives easier becomes an afterthought.

Understanding Customers' Needs

If you start with the customer, the customer can't be an afterthought. The way I expressed this to my colleagues was to say, "Strategic relevance is all from the consumer back." And conveniently, we had new research to consult on the subject of consumer needs. Whirlpool and Sears had recently engaged Boston Consulting Group to study consumers' desires with regard to appliance delivery. The top-line finding was that people value what I call "delivery with integrity." That is, your ability to get it there fast is important, but not as important as your ability to get it there when you said you would. "Give a date, hit a date" is what they're asking for. This sounded familiar to me, coming from the automotive industry. In my previous position at General Motors, I'd been involved in several studies that emphasized the psychology of delivery date commitments.

Identifying Trade Partners' Priorities

Moving upstream, we needed to understand the desires of our direct customers better. We conducted our own interviews to define requirements by segment. As well as looking at smaller retailers versus larger ones, we focused individually on Sears, Lowes, and Best Buy, our three biggest customers. And within the contract-builder market, we studied many subdivisions, from contract distributors and apartment developers to single-family-home builders. We asked about their overall availability requirements, their preferences in communicating with us, and what they would like to see along the lines of e-business. We asked about inventory management and how they might want Whirlpool to assist in it. In all, we discovered 27 different dimensions along which our performance was being judged, each varying in importance according to the customer.

Benchmarking the Competition

Naturally, our customers' expectations and perceptions were shaped in large part by what others in our industry were doing. So we benchmarked our competitors—primarily GE, which was our biggest rival. We obtained cross-industry information and competitive intelligence from AMR, Gartner, and Forrester Research to make sure we had a broad and objective assessment of supply chain capabilities. Then we mapped out what would be considered world-class (versus sufficient or transitional) performance for each of the 27 capabilities and how much it would cost us to reach that top level. It turned out that to prevail on every front would require a total investment of more than $85 million, which we knew wasn't feasible. It was time to get serious about priorities.

Now that we had established the cost of world-beating performance, we asked ourselves: For each capability, what improvement could we accomplish at a low investment level, and at a medium level? We quickly staked out the areas where a relatively small investment would yield supremacy, usually due to an existing strength. A few areas we simply decided to cede. Our plan was to meet or beat the competition in most areas, at minimum cost.

Building for the Future

Strategy, of course, does not simply address the needs of the moment. It anticipates the challenges of the future. A final component of our supply chain strategy was identifying the probable range of future operating scenarios based on industry, economic, and technological trends. The point was to assure ourselves that our proposal was robust enough to withstand these various scenarios. To date, the planning has worked. Having set a course, we've been able to deal with situations we hadn't conceived of and to continue evolving in the same basic direction.

Selling the Revolution

It's always a difficult decision—when to involve your internal customers in the planning of a major capital investment. Their time is scarce, and they typically don't want to be embroiled in the details of what you, after all, are getting paid to do. You must have your act together and have a solid plan to which they can respond. On the other hand, you can't be so far along in the process that you've become inflexible. You need to maintain a careful balance between seeking their guidance and selling your vision.

Paul and I liked to think we had that mandate from Jeff Fettig to get the supply chain fixed. But it wasn't the kind of mandate that comes with a blank check. Like most well-managed companies, Whirlpool will not undertake a capital investment without a compelling business case. As a cost center in the company, we had to justify our project wholly on expense reductions and working capital improvements. Even if we believed that better product availability would boost sales, we couldn't count those chickens in the business case.

We spent an enormous amount of time talking with the brand general managers and others who would be affected by the changes we were proposing. The Japanese call this kind of consensus-building *nemawashi* (literally, it means "root binding"), and it is impossible to overstate its importance. Yet it is often neglected in the midst of a complex project. Note that, at the same time we needed to be meeting with key decision makers, we were also in the thick of the analysis and design of the solution. In those early months, the project needed leadership in two directions—the kind of work people typically refer to as needing a "Mr. Inside" and "Mr. Outside." I made sure we had sufficient consulting resources for the inside work while Paul and I devoted 50% of our time to the outside work—interfacing with the trade, outside experts, and internal stakeholders.

In our initial meetings with these key people, we'd essentially say, "Here's what we're doing. What do you think?" Typically, the executive would half pay attention, half blow us off. But we'd get some input. In a second meeting, we'd show how our work had evolved to incorporate their ideas and others'. Usually, we'd see more engagement at this point. By the time we were asking for a third meeting, reactions were mixed. People were more or less on board, but some felt another meeting wasn't needed. They said they had nothing more to add. But we persisted. I remember telling Paul, "If they won't let us in the door, we'll go through the window. And if they lock the window, there's always the air vent. . . ."

Along the way, we'd been particularly concerned about cherry-picking. We knew that, in a company of smart businesspeople, the first reaction to a multimillion-dollar price tag would be, "OK, what can I get for 80% of that total?" And indeed, from a project management standpoint, we knew it was important to break out each component of the plan into a stand-alone initiative, justified by its own business case. Yet we knew the whole thing came together as a sort of basket weave, with each part supporting and relying on multiple other parts.

What helped here was our competitive analysis, in which we had plotted our capability levels against others'. We charted our current position against our number one competitor on each dimension valued by customers, then extrapolated to show how, depending on the level of investment, we could overtake that company or allow the gap to widen. Sure enough, the competitive instincts of our colleagues kicked in. No one wanted to fall behind.

Getting Focused

One of the earliest successes in the turnaround of Whirlpool's supply chain was the rollout of a new sales and operations planning (S&OP) process. Our previous planning environment had been inadequate. What passed for planning tools didn't go far beyond Excel spreadsheets. Now, we had the ability to pull together the long-term and short-term perspectives of marketing, sales, finance, and manufacturing and produce forecasts that all the participants could base their game plans on.

We soon pushed our forecasting capability further by launching a CPFR pilot. The acronym stands for collaborative planning, forecasting, and replenishment, with the collaboration happening across different companies within a supply chain. The idea is straightforward. Traditionally, we forecast how many appliances we will sell through a trade partner (Sears, for example) to a given market. And at the same time, that trade partner develops its own forecast. Each of us has some information that the other lacks. With CPFR, we use a Web-based tool to share our forecasts (without sharing the sensitive data behind them), and we collaborate on the exceptions. As simple as it sounds, it isn't easy to pull off. But we have, and it's been a real home run. Within 30 days of launch, our forecast accuracy error was cut in half. Where we had close to 100% error (which isn't hard, given the small quantities involved in forecasting individual SKUs for specific warehouse locations), today we're at about 44% or 45%. To put this in perspective, a one-point improvement in forecast accuracy across the board reduces our total finished goods position by several million dollars.

These were just two of many initiatives we launched in rapid succession after May 2001. A couple things were absolutely critical to keeping them all on track: a highly disciplined project management office and stringent performance metrics. The key was to think big but focus relentlessly on near-term deadlines. We organized the change effort into 30-day chunks, with three new capabilities, or business releases, rolling out monthly—some on the supply side, some on the demand side.

The job of the project management office was to ensure the completion of projects on time, on budget, and on benefit. Paul oversaw this for me. Also keeping us honest were new metrics—and the man I brought in to enforce them. My colleague John Kerr, now general manager of quality for the North America division, was then in charge of Whirlpool's Six Sigma program. He's a real black belt when it comes to performance management. It took some persuading, aimed at both John and the North American leadership team, before he was freed up and allowed to dedicate himself to the supply chain turnaround. But we absolutely needed his data-driven perspective. When one of my team would say, "We need to take this action to fix this issue," John would always counter with, "Please show me the data that allowed you to draw that conclusion." Were these demands sometimes a source of irritation? I'd be lying if I said they weren't. But they forced all of us to rebuild the metric "fact base" and hone our problem-solving skills.

By the third quarter of 2001, we had already done a lot to stabilize product availability and reduce overall supply chain costs. And, after a challenging fourth quarter, we took a huge step forward by implementing a suite of software products from i2, which specializes in supply chain integration tools. That was in January 2002. Six months later, Whirlpool had historic low inventories and a sustained high service level. Before the year was out, we were delivering very near our target of 93% availability across all brands and products. (Momentum has since carried us well into the mid-nineties.) We delivered slightly more than promised by reducing finished goods working capital by 10% and improving total cost productivity by 5.1%.

Our customers were voicing their approval. By May 2002, a blind Internet survey given to our trade partners showed us to be "most improved," "easiest to do business with," and "most progressive." I remember that after these results came out, our VP of sales said, "You're good now—but more important, you're *consistently* good." It was a turning point in the trade's perception of Whirlpool.

Engaging Talent

I've touched on the state-of-the-art technologies we've employed in our turnaround—the Web-based collaboration tools, the planning software, i2's rocket-science optimization—but let me correct any impression that this is a story about technology. More than anything, Whirlpool's supply chain turnaround is a talent renaissance.

It's sometimes hard for us to remember how demoralized this 3,000-person organization had become. In 2000, many people in supply chain roles had been with the company for years and had watched in frustration as competitors outspent and outperformed us. Part of the problem was the massive effort required by the ERP implementation. As an early adopter of enterprise systems in our industry (SAP and other vendors got their start with process-manufacturing concerns like industrial chemicals), Whirlpool had bitten off a lot. With limited attention and resources to spare, it put other projects on hold. We took our eye off the ball in supply chain innovation and fell behind.

As a newcomer, I tried to inject some fresh energy into the organization and give people a reason to be confident. Paul Dittmann told me this project gave him a "second career wind." He's a brilliant guy, with a PhD in operations research and industrial engineering, and suddenly, he had the opportunity to innovate in ways he had only dreamed of in his first 20 years at the company.

Other people benefited from changes to how we develop, assess, and reward talent. With help from Michigan State University and the American Production and Inventory Control Society (APICS), we developed a supply chain "competency model." This is essentially an outline of the skills required in a top-tier organization, the roles in which they should reside, and how they need to be developed over time. And we created a new banding system, which expanded the compensation levels in the organization. Now people can be rewarded for increasing their expertise even if they are not being promoted into supervisory roles.

We also put a heavy emphasis on developing people's project management skills. Here, we relied on a model developed by the Project Management Institute (PMI), a sort of standard for assessing and enhancing an organization's project management capabilities. I wanted as many supply chain professionals as possible to become PMI-certified, and not just because of the glut of projects we were facing at the moment. My view is that project management's disciplined planning and execution is just as vital to ongoing operations management. After all, the only real difference between running an operation and running a project is the due date of the deliverable. Over time, my operating staff stopped dismissing project management as a lot of "overhead" from a former management consultant and car guy. Now they're the ones insisting on things like project charters and weekly project reviews.

Meanwhile, we hired at least 13 new people on the business side and at least as many more on the information systems side, and I made sure that every one of them was top-notch. To fill out our project management ranks, we recruited young people from companies with strong supply chains and from premier operations-oriented MBA programs like Michigan State and the University of Tennessee. Perhaps we were lucky that our talent drive coincided with a downturn in the consulting industry. On the other hand, it might have been the excitement of a turnaround situation that drew the best and brightest to Whirlpool.

Finally, I wasn't so arrogant as to believe that my senior team and I didn't need development ourselves. We assembled a supply chain advisory board and chartered its members to keep challenging us. The group includes academics Don Bowersox of Michigan State and Tom Mentzer of the University of Tennessee, and practitioners Ralph Drayer (the Procter & Gamble executive who pioneered Efficient Consumer Response) and Larry Sur (who mastered transportation and warehouse management in a long career at Schneider National and GENCO). Get a group like this together, and you can count on creative sparks flying. These experts keep us on our toes in a way no consulting firm could.

Sustaining Momentum

Three years into the project now, we continue to assign ourselves and deliver three new capabilities per month. This doesn't get simpler over time, either. As I write this, for example, we're focused on something we call "Plan to Sell/Build to Order." Here, the notion is that certain high-volume SKUs should never be out of stock. These are the heart-of-the-line dishwashers, refrigerators, washing machines, and other products that appeal to a broad range of consumers. They are the equivalent of a supermarket's milk and eggs; running out of them has a disproportionately negative impact on customers' perceptions.

We're now formulating a supply chain strategy that allows us to identify these SKUs across all of our trade partners in all of our channels and to ensure that the replenishment system for our regional warehouses keeps them in stock. That constitutes the "plan to sell" part of the program. At the same time, for our smallest-volume SKUs, we are taking out all the inventory and operating on a pure pull basis, with a new, more flexible build-to-order process. The inventory savings on the small-volume SKUs helps offset the costs of stocking up on the high-volume SKUs.

We're also working on the capability to set service levels by SKU. That is, instead of having one availability target for all our products, we are recognizing that some products are of greater strategic importance than others. Some of them, for instance, are more profitable. Some hold a unique place in our brand strategy. Again, it's easy to grasp the value of being able to vary service levels accordingly. But in a sprawling business like ours, shipping thousands of different SKUs daily, it's a very difficult thing to accomplish.

We continue to develop new Web-based tools. Recently, we've been focused on system-to-system transactions, in which our system talks directly to a customer's system for purposes of transmitting orders, exchanging sales data, and even submitting and paying invoices. We've rolled out this capability with a number of trade partners over the past 18 months. At the same time, we keep enhancing our Partner Store, which allows customers to check availability and place orders via the Internet. The site allows them to find near equivalents of models, for those times when a SKU is out of stock or retired. They can even find deals on obsolete inventory.

By the time this article appears in print, we'll also have implemented event-management technology, which will allow us to be more on top of the movement of goods through the supply chain. An event manager provides an alert whenever an action in the process has taken place—for example, when a washer is loaded into a container in Schorndorf, when that container full of washers is loaded onto a ship in Rotterdam, when the ship departs, when the ship arrives, when the container is unloaded from the ship in Norfolk, when the container leaves the port via truck, and, finally, when the washer is unloaded at the Findlay, Ohio, warehouse. The result is that people's attention is directed to what needs to be done. We'll also be further along in our application of lean techniques (usually associated with manufacturing operations) to our total supply chain. This involves using pull concepts and kanbanlike triggers to speed up processes, reduce inventory, and enhance customer service.

On the Horizon

Whirlpool has much to show for its supply chain efforts. By the end of 2003, our product availability had reached over 93%, up from 88.3% in 2001. (Today it's more than 95%.) That allowed us to attain an order fill rate for key trade partners of over 96%. The number of days' worth of finished goods we were holding in inventory had dropped from 32.8 to just 26. We drove freight and warehousing total cost productivity from 4% to 7.2%. From 2002 to 2003, we lowered working capital by almost $100 million and supply chain costs by almost $20 million. Does all this add up to value in excess of the expense our leadership team approved? Absolutely. In fact, total payback on that original investment occurred within the first two years.

Still, our work is far from finished. In October 2001, just months after we kicked off our turnaround, we were fortunate in that the new executive vice president brought in to run Whirlpool's North America region had deep supply chain knowledge. Dave Swift, who came to us from Kodak, believes strongly in the strategic importance of the supply chain both for building brands and for creating sustainable competitive advantage. Immediately after joining us, he elevated our sales and operations planning process by personally chairing monthly executive S&OP meetings. These meetings have become the model for the company and the basis for much of our just-started global supply chain efforts.

In the future, we'll face greater demands for end-to-end accountability. We're already responsible for the resale of any returns. Soon we'll be accountable for the disassembly of products in Europe. It's only a matter of time before similar laws are enacted in the United States.

And we'll be taking an even closer look at the design of the products themselves. If we can redesign a product—make it in a smaller plant, make it with smaller parts, ship it in smaller pieces—we can dramatically affect supply chain economics. It's great to improve forecasts, optimize transportation, and speed up our processes with existing SKUs. But what if we could push the end stages of production closer to the consumer and get higher leverage from those SKUs? That's the kind of thing that can change the rules of the game.

It's a wonderful thing about our business: We have fierce competition all over the world, and on top of that we have very smart trade partners who deal with numerous other suppliers. We may be a white goods, big box supplier, but because our customers also buy electronics and apparel and so on, we're constantly being challenged by the benchmarks of other, more nimble industries. Technologies continue to evolve, channel power continues to shift, and the bar is constantly being raised. But I'm confident that the talent in Whirlpool's supply chain organization will be equal to it all.

REUBEN E. SLONE is the vice president of global supply chain at Whirlpool.

Originally published in October 2004. Reprint R0410G

Index

partnerships and, 138–139, 147
silos and, 179–180
trust and, 183–184
Michigan State University,
208–209
microfinancing, 6
Microsoft, 58–59, 191
Tag codes, 26, 29
Morris, Sandra, 174, 176, 179,
185, 189
Mrs. Fields, 103
mu-chips, 24
mutuality, 141, 142–143

National Bicycle, 124–126
nemawashi, 203–204
Nestlé, 31
Nike, 1, 9
Nokia, 53–54, 56

OfficeMax, 81
Old Navy, 60
online-verification codes, 25–26
operating controls, 146, 147
Operation Safe Commerce, 191
organization
functional silos and, 172,
178–181
partnerships and compatibility of, 141–146
rapid-fire fulfillment and, 160
Ortega, Amancio, 153, 157, 168

Panasonic, 124–126
partnership model, 131–152
action items and time frames
in, 146–150
drivers session in, 137–141
evaluating potential in,
139–140

frank discussion in, 135, 137
justification of partnerships
in, 132–135
organizational compatibility
in, 141–146
propensity-to-partner matrix
in, 144–145
versatility of, 150–152
Partner Store, 211
Pepsi, 143
performance, 180–181. *See also*
metrics
Pessina, Michael W., 125–126
planning, 77, 89–90
adaptive strategy in, 173–174
execution vs., 174–175
partnerships and, 146
short-term thinking and,
77, 90–96
supply-chain strategy, 109–113
Plan to Sell/Build to Order,
210–211
PlayStation 2, 59
Posco, 5, 7–8, 10
postponement, 55, 165
pricing, efficiency and, 118–122
priorities, 200–201
Prius, 61–62
processes
lean, 85–86
sustainable, 7
Procter & Gamble, 12, 102, 116
products
designing and rapid fulfillment, 158–162, 213–214
designing for adaptability, 63
designing for agility, 55
development of at Seven-
Eleven Japan, 71
functional vs. innovative,
101–129
labeling, 23–25, 28–29

You don't want to miss these...

We've combed through hundreds of *Harvard Business Review* articles on key management topics and selected *the* most important ones to help you maximize your own and your organization's performance.

10 Must-Read Articles on:

LEADERSHIP
How can you transform yourself from a good manager into an extraordinary leader?

STRATEGY
Is your company spending an enormous amount of time and energy on strategy development, with little to show for its efforts?

MANAGING YOURSELF
The path to your own professional success starts with a critical look in the mirror.

CHANGE
70 percent of all change initiatives fail. Learn how to turn the odds in your company's favor.

MANAGING PEOPLE
What really motivates people? How do you deal with problem employees? How can you build a team that is greater than the sum of its parts?

THE ESSENTIALS
If you read nothing else, read these 10 articles from some of *Harvard Business Review*'s most influential authors.

Harvard Business Review Press